paint your life
a brighter shade of
green

paint your life
a brighter shade of
green

carolyn humphries

foulsham
LONDON • NEW YORK • TORONTO • SYDNEY

foulsham

The Publishing House, Bennetts Close, Cippenham,
Slough, Berkshire, SL1 5AP, England

Foulsham books can be found in all good bookshops and direct from
www.foulsham.com

ISBN: 978-0-572-03450-4

Copyright © 2008 Carolyn Humphries

Cover photographs © Superstock and iStock

A CIP record for this book is available from the British Library

The moral right of the author has been asserted

While every effort has been made to ensure the
accuracy of all the information contained within this
book, neither the author nor the publisher can be liable
for any errors. In particular, since technology and
ecological awareness are advancing all the time, it is
vital that each individual checks relevant details for
themselves. This book is offered as a guide only.

Printed in Great Britain by Creative Print and Design (Wales), Ebbw Vale

Contents

Introduction

Every country in the world is aware of the problems our planet is facing. Global warming won't simply go away. Arguments rage about what has caused it and who is to blame but the bottom line is, if every one of us doesn't do something about it, our planet will be destroyed.

There is no easy fix, of course, but governments worldwide are beginning to take steps – some in much bigger strides than others – to reduce emissions and work towards a greener future. Government legislation is not enough, though; if we, as individuals, all do a little bit, our small steps can make a difference. The answer to questions like *'how can what I do in my home affect the habitat of polar bears on a different continent?'* is that whatever we do anywhere on this planet has an impact on everyone and everything. Each country isn't an isolated bubble that operates entirely on its own; we all breath the same atmosphere, are surrounded by the same ozone layer and need the same basics for survival.

I am neither a scientist nor a politician – I am someone who, just like you, is trying to make sense of the conflicting arguments and information that bombard us all the time so that I can do my bit to go greener. In this book I've looked at the issues and tried to interpret them in a simple and clear way to help us understand the reasons why we all have to change our lifestyles and go greener and also to encourage all of us to rethink what we do on a daily

basis. In the eyes of experts, I may not have got it all exactly right but the overall message is loud and clear – everyone must take action. You'll find lots of practical help and easy steps to better ways to do everything – from recycling waste to heating and lighting your home, shopping more responsibly and even ways to cook to save fuel and to use up leftovers instead of throwing them away.

There are, of course, enormous pros to going green – but there are some cons too. It takes a little time and effort and, in some cases, some financial input to become seriously eco-friendly. It isn't cut and dried or easy either. For every positive, there can be a negative, though I firmly believe the plusses outweigh the minuses. That may all sound off-putting to some but you don't have to turn into the stereotypical tree-hugging hippie to care about the environment nor do you have to be a millionaire. Every one of us – young and old alike – can contribute in some way and here's where to find out what you can do and how even making little changes can mean so much. You can select the ones that work for you and you'll be pleased to discover that in many instances you won't have to shell out your hard-earned cash, but may actually save your money as well as the world's resources.

This book is designed to be straightforward and useful. It begins with a chapter outlining the growth in awareness of green issues, the current situation and what the term 'carbon footprint' actually means – the serious scientific stuff, which is not only very useful to know but will strengthen your determination to do your bit to save the planet. However, you can skip this chapter if you prefer (and want to get started straight away) and go on to the following ones, which each cover a green topic and provide advice on the practical things you can do at home, in the shops, and in all the main areas of your life to lessen your carbon footprint and make your life greener.

1

What's it all about?

Climate change is probably the biggest problem facing our planet. You could argue – and many do – that there have been oscillating weather patterns throughout the earth's history. Over the last 900,000 years it has fluctuated between cold glacial periods and the much warmer interglacial periods, one of which we are in now. There have also been times when the weather has rapidly become hotter and wetter but then plummeted into an ice age (the last ice age ended about 10,000 years ago). However, although some scientists had predicted that another ice age was therefore almost inevitable some time in the foreseeable future (though they couldn't say when), many now believe that the chances are very remote.

The main reasons for this change of mind are that the burning of fossil fuels over the past 200 years or so, coupled with increased industrial processing (such as the manufacture of cement) plus deforestation – the felling of trees to make way for towns, housing and roads as well as to use for fuel, paper, furniture, utensils and other products – have created a huge increase in carbon dioxide emissions. This has caused an unprecedented rise in climate temperature that could eventually lead to the destruction of the planet. It's not just carbon dioxide either; modern life has caused an increase in several other gases that all add to this greenhouse effect, which I shall discuss later.

The main point is that we must act now to change our lifestyles in order to, at the very least, slow up the process of global warming. Obviously, the ultimate aim should be to redress the balance.

The totally selfish among us will argue that there is no point in trying to change our lifestyles if we are going to melt or freeze eventually anyway – we may as well enjoy ourselves and to heck with the consequences. After all, *we* won't be around when the time comes. They might also argue that it's too late to undo the damage we have already done.

I don't agree with these attitudes. While it's true that no one can know how, if or when life on this planet, as we know it, might reach total disaster, I believe we can try to slow down the destruction *and* make our environment as pleasant as possible. And maybe, just maybe, we can save it altogether! We can, most certainly, try.

There are plenty of ways in which all of us can help make this planet a more environmentally friendly place, as you will see through this book. It will improve quality of life worldwide – and not just for the wealthy industrialised nations; developing countries, too, will benefit from projects set up now, as you'll read later in this chapter, and from the implementation of fair trade across the globe (see Fair Food and Clothing for a Fair Price, page 54).

Short-term, practical measures are possible. For instance, because of our disposable society, the amount of man-made waste we produce is just too much for the planet to cope with. We have very few landfill sites left and those that are already full emit unacceptable amounts of methane. This is a potent gas that contributes more even than carbon dioxide to global warming (see The Greenhouse Gases, page 12). Not only that, unless we commit to the existing measures to curb our waste, we'll all be living cheek by jowl with it – back to the times of rubbish piling up in the streets, vermin infestations and disease. Also, we are running out of fossil fuels so we need to conserve energy and find more environmentally friendly alternatives to them. We can and are doing something about that too (see Chapter 9, page 117).

Are we really experiencing a climate change?

A recent report from the Intergovernmental Panel on Climate Change (IPCC) stated that evidence is now unequivocal that global temperatures are rising and we are 90 per cent responsible for it. There have been observed global increases in ocean and air temperatures, with the land warming faster than the sea. The years of the last decade (in their words, 11 of the last 12 years) rank among the 12 warmest since records began in 1850. Sea levels have risen on average 1.8 mm a year since 1993, due in part to thermal expansion and melting snow caps, glaciers and polar ice sheets. If this is allowed to continue, the projected rise by the end of this century is 18–59 cm! There is less snow globally too. The frozen Arctic sea has melted by 2.7 per cent per decade since 1978 in winter and a staggering 7.4 per cent per decade in summer.

Many parts of the world have experienced significant increases in rainfall but there are pockets where severe drought has increased. There are indications that hot days and nights have increased over the last 50 years, with frosts and cold spells becoming less frequent. More tropical cyclones have been observed in the North Atlantic, though there is only limited evidence of increases elsewhere.

Stark warnings

This report gave stark warnings of what the future will hold if we don't all make an enormous effort to redress the balance. It said that many plant and wildlife species will face extinction and food and water shortages could affect hundreds of millions more people. Heat waves, storms, droughts, floods and land erosion are likely to increase too. The shocking thing is that the report was referring not to a situation in hundreds of years' time, but over the next few decades! Sadly, too, the poorer countries, whose contribution to global warming is much less significant than that of the more affluent countries, are likely to suffer the worst effects.

The greenhouse effect

The greenhouse effect works like this. The earth is warmed by the sun. Only some of the solar rays penetrate the earth's atmosphere and reach the surface. As the surface warms it radiates its own infrared rays of heat. The greenhouse gases, trapped in the

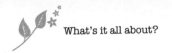

atmosphere, absorb the heat and warm the earth even more. Without greenhouse gases, the earth would be considerably colder than it is now. If we create more greenhouse gases, more heat will be absorbed and the earth will get hotter – and that's what global warming is.

The greenhouse gases

It's worth knowing what the greenhouse gases are if you are going to understand fully what is thought to be happening.

Most of the earth's atmosphere is made up of nitrogen and oxygen, which we need to sustain life but they don't affect the climate as such. The most prevalent greenhouse gas is carbon dioxide; the other significant ones are methane, nitrous oxide, halocarbons, ozone and water vapour.

Carbon dioxide

Billions of years ago, there was a great deal of carbon dioxide in the atmosphere but most of it was taken out by micro-organisms and trapped in the earth's crust in the form of carbonate minerals, petroleum, oil, shale and coal. Now it is created by decaying plants, and also by volcanoes, as well as being breathed out by animals, including humans. It is absorbed by plants during photosynthesis and it dissolves in water – the seas, lakes and rivers. For millions of years roughly the same amount of carbon dioxide was created naturally as was absorbed, which maintained a fine balance. However, since we discovered the coal, oil, petroleum and so on in the earth's crust and started burning them as fuel, and felled so many of the trees that absorbed carbon dioxide – and burned them too – we've allowed an excess of it back into the atmosphere and destroyed that natural balance. This excess carbon dioxide will stay in the atmosphere for about 100 years, absorbing the heat from the earth.

Methane

Methane is produced by bacteria in the gut of animals and in rotting matter and is also a natural gas found in the earth's crust. It is removed from the atmosphere by a chemical reaction to form water vapour. The balance here has been upset by the vast increase in livestock farming, and also by rice fields, which provide the ideal warm, wet conditions for bacteria to produce methane. All the rotting waste in landfill sites also produces methane. It stays in the atmosphere for about 12 years. Although there is far less methane than carbon dioxide, its warming effect is much greater.

Nitrous oxide

Nitrous oxide is naturally formed by micro-organisms in the soil that extract the nitrogen and release it back into the atmosphere, forming nitrous oxide. It is also put into the atmosphere by the oceans. The naturally occurring amount is small, but our burning of fossil fuels and wood and use of nitrogen-based fertilizers has produced far more. It remains in the atmosphere for as much as 150 years and is extremely powerful at retaining heat.

Halocarbons

Halocarbons are, arguably, the worst of the greenhouse gases because they don't occur naturally but are man-made. Chlorofluorocarbons (CFCs) are probably the best known. They were used in aerosol sprays, cleaners and solvents until the 1980s when it was realised how damaging they were to the ozone layer (see below). They were replaced with hydrofluorocarbons (HFCs), which are believed to be less harmful to the ozone layer. Unfortunately, they still get trapped in the atmosphere (as they don't break up naturally) and are likely to remain for three or four hundred years so still contribute to the greenhouse effect.

Ozone

We've all heard of the ozone layer, a natural part of the earth's atmosphere. This layer is in the outer part of the atmosphere – the stratosphere – and protects the earth from the sun's harmful ultraviolet rays. Holes in this layer caused by the use of hydrocarbons, among other things, is thought to have allowed more harmful ultraviolet (UV) rays to reach the earth. However, the ozone also traps the infrared rays from the earth, causing the greenhouse effect, though the extent compared with carbon dioxide is not known. Ozone nearer the ground is a pollutant, too. This poisonous gas is formed when sunlight reacts with nitrous oxide or halocarbons in the air – the first steps to smog – which is damaging to lungs and affects plant growth. So, while industrial smoke and exhaust fumes don't contain ozone, they do create it. It's a double-edged sword: we need ozone to protect us from the sun's harmful rays but too much is damaging to health. Ozone is constantly being created and destroyed so there isn't really a timeline on it.

Water vapour

Water vapour is the largest contributor to the greenhouse effect. It breaks down in the stratosphere, releasing hydrogen oxide that

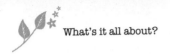

destroys the ozone layer and so lets in more of the sun's rays, including harmful UV ones. Warm air holds more water vapour than cold (that's why tropical countries are far more humid that cold ones), so the warmer the earth gets, the more water vapour will be held in the atmosphere and the warmer (and wetter) it will get and the more the ozone layer will be destroyed – a vicious circle. Methane is also turned into water vapour in the stratosphere, adding to the wetter conditions and destruction of the ozone layer.

Obviously we can't undo the creating of greenhouse gases in the past but, as they don't stay in the atmosphere for ever, we can reduce them in the future and try to redress the balance.

Reducing carbon emissions – what the world is doing

As I write this book, things are changing. It's important to give you some background and to bring you up to where we are now.

The Kyoto Protocol

The United Nations Framework Convention on Climate Change (UNFCCC) was set up in 1994. It is pretty much universal – 192 countries ratified it. Governments agreed to share information, best practices and policies on greenhouse gas emissions; to share strategies for cutting greenhouse emissions; and to offer technological and financial support to developing countries and to help each other prepare and adapt to the impacts of climate change. An extension to this is the Kyoto Protocol, an international agreement drawn up in Kyoto, Japan, in 1997, which agreed more definite and legally binding measures to cut worldwide greenhouse gas emissions. Developed countries had to commit to reduce their carbon emissions by levels agreed for each of them between 2008 and 2012 to add up to a worldwide reduction of 5 per cent compared with 1990. They also had to produce a Greenhouse Gas Inventory every year. Developed nations have to make more changes because they have contributed most to the problem and they can more easily afford to do so.

Three incentives

Three incentives are in place to try to ensure countries can meet the targets – Emissions Trading, Joint Implementation and the

Clean Development Mechanism. These encourage private sector companies in developed countries to work on projects with developing countries and they can earn and trade emissions credits when they do so. This also helps them find the most cost-effective way of reducing emissions. The mechanisms, in turn, help developing countries get the technology and investment they require to grow. Developing countries, on the other hand, don't contribute so highly to global warming so they aren't expected to *cut* their emissions but are allowed to *increase* them in line with the global policy when they participate in the scheme. This doesn't just mean third world countries, though; China and India are also included because they were underdeveloped at the time of the industrialisation period that is thought to have caused the greenhouse effect in the first place. Both countries are fully aware of the situation and say they share the commitment to reduce emissions in the future.

The signatories

As I understand it, by June 2007, 172 countries (including the European Union as one) had signed the agreement. By November 2007, of those signatories only Australia, the USA and Kazakhstan had not ratified it. The USA refused because it would have to cut emissions by 7 per cent below its 1990 emissions by 2012 and it would not do that unless China and other rapidly developing countries were included in the agreement. President Bush also declined because he feared it would damage the US economy.

The next step

There has been a very recent development. In December 2007 the UNFCCC met in Bali, Indonesia, with representatives from more than 180 countries. After a rocky ride, with only the USA holding out to the eleventh hour, the conference adopted the Bali Roadmap, which charts a course for negotiations, aimed to conclude in 2009, that will then lay down an international agreement on climate change for post-2012 (when the current Kyoto Protocol expires). The conference did manage some innovative resolutions that will form the basis of the future agreement: an Adaptation Fund (to allow developing countries, which are most vulnerable to the effects of climate change, to receive funding to help them adapt) and also decisions on deforestation and the transfer of technology from the developed countries to the developing ones.

The UK's commitment – the good news

According to National Statistics, under the Kyoto Protocol, the UK is legally bound to reduce emissions of the six main greenhouse gases to 12.5 per cent below those of 1990 by 2008–2012. It is estimated that by 2004 they were down 14.6 per cent. Carbon dioxide emissions were down 5.6 per cent.

The government has passed a bill committing the UK to reducing carbon emissions by between 26 and 32 per cent by 2020 and a 60 per cent reduction by 2050. This makes the UK the first nation to actually lay it down in law. However, many environmentalists think this doesn't go far enough and say that an 80 per cent cut is needed by 2050. At least we are moving in the right direction and the Prime Minister has stated that he will still look to see if bigger cuts are required.

Government initiatives

The Carbon Emissions Reduction Target (Cert) obligation requires energy suppliers to make consumers' homes more energy efficient. In support of this, the government is providing £100 million to the Energy Saving Trust to deliver a broader programme for greener homes to try to stop the worst consequences of climate change. It will provide a network of advice centres, particularly work with the over 70s and those on low income, and give over 100 neighbourhoods – concentrating on homes where it is difficult to reduce the carbon footprint – a green makeover to show them how to reduce their carbon footprints by more than 60 per cent. There is also an *Act on CO_2 Advice Line* to give people a 'one-stop shop' for all their environmental needs. This is on the same number as your Energy Saving Trust local advice centre number (see page 152).

The APPCDC

The Kyoto Protocol isn't the only agreement in place at the moment. The Asia-Pacific Partnership on Clean Development and Climate (APPCDC) is an international agreement launched in 2006 by Australia, South Korea, India, China, Japan and the USA. These countries agreed to co-operate in the development and transfer of technology to reduce greenhouse gas emissions. Canada has also joined recently. The difference between it and the Kyoto Protocol is that there are no mandatory targets; the countries involved set their own goals. The plus side is that these member countries actually produce well over half the entire world's carbon emissions so, if they work together, they could make a significant difference. Also, under Kyoto, India and China did not have to cut emissions, but with this agreement they do.

However, critics of the APPCDC say that, because there are no targets, the partnership doesn't amount to anything except good intentions. The biggest danger is that the APPCDC could become an anti-Kyoto bloc. What we need is for all countries to recognise how much they contribute to the overall greenhouse gases and to agree to work together to cut emissions accordingly as efficiently and as quickly as possible. We still have a long way to go.

Why should we bother when some countries produce so much carbon?

The USA is responsible for nearly a quarter of the world's greenhouse gases. President Bush has finally agreed that it is a 'serious problem' requiring 'urgent action'. Having rejected the Kyoto Protocol, he has proposed a climate change initiative calling for, among other things, voluntary emission reductions and new research into alternative fuels. Individual states, such as California, are implementing their own policies.

Developing countries like China are victims of their own success. China has one of the most rapidly rising economies, which has increased wealth and produced general health benefits but has, conversely, suffered from horrendous levels of pollution as a result of industrialisation and the burning of coal: acid rain is now falling on 30 per cent of the land and its emissions have doubled since 1980 along with its economic growth. For the first time ever, China has overtaken the USA as the world's largest carbon dioxide emitter. This has been a real wake-up call to the world's politicians and means the incentive to find a universal agreement, that all countries will ratify, is imperative by 2012 when the current Kyoto Protocol expires.

The Chinese government recognises the implications of global warming. It is a member of the APPCDC and recently announced its first national plan to reduce or avoid greenhouse gas emissions. Modern technology and cost are two major issues for China in implementing such a strategy. At present it relies heavily on coal for fuel, and Chinese industries are not yet prepared to use unproven alternatives. They need international support and help to facilitate change. China has a growing cement industry too – a large contributor to carbon dioxide emissions. At present other greenhouse gases have not been monitored but, as we already know that rice fields produce large amounts of methane, there is a lot of work to be done.

Taking these facts into consideration, it means that the USA and China, between them, produce almost half of the world's greenhouse gas emissions. But they do recognise that fact and will gradually implement changes. Everyone has to take a positive role – it's a *global* reduction that has to happen as soon as possible and, even if America and China are currently lagging behind Europe and Russia, the pressure is on for all nations and every individual to be proactive.

A step back?

With all this going on globally, I have just discovered that plans have been passed by a council in Kent to build a coal-fuelled power plant – the first for 20 years. If the government approves the plans, in my opinion this is a serious retrograde step. How can we, as part of the developed world, accuse countries like China and India of over-using fossil fuels for industry if we choose to do the same?

Are we doomed either way?

My honest answer is 'I hope not' but, according to Dr James Lovelock, it may be the case. He developed the Gaia Theory, in the late 1960s, that organic and inorganic components of the earth have evolved together to work as one self-regulating living system: 'Life maintains conditions suitable for its own survival.' In other words, it adapts according to the conditions. He believes that, considering the earth like this, when carbon dioxide emissions exceed a certain level, the temperature rises by 6°C and then stabilises again. This is different from the IPCC idea that the earth's temperature will rise and fall evenly according to the amount of carbon dioxide in the atmosphere. However, at a recent lecture on climate change, Dr Lovelock warned that a quick reduction in greenhouse emissions could actually speed up global warming. He believes that 'global dimming' is currently offsetting global warming. The industrial pollution in the atmosphere is reducing the earth's temperature by 2–3°C (presumably because the density of the gases prevents the sun's rays penetrating) but if we stopped the burning of fossil fuels it might get hotter. That is pretty much doomed if you do, doomed if you don't.

Your carbon footprint

We all need to stop creating so much carbon dioxide and other greenhouse gases, but you may wonder how we can know what we are using. The carbon footprint measures the impact each individual's activities has on the environment in terms of how many units of carbon dioxide are produced.

The footprint is divided into two parts. The primary footprint measures direct emissions from fossil fuel burning; this includes transport and domestic fuel for heating, lighting and cooking. The secondary footprint measures indirect emissions from the products we use, from their manufacture through to their disposal.

Below is a pie chart, based on one from carbonfootprint.com, that shows you an average person's carbon footprint.

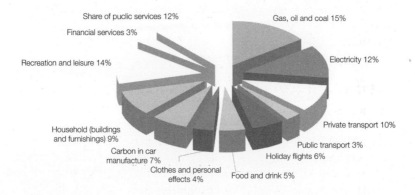

Share of puclic services 12%
Financial services 3%
Recreation and leisure 14%
Household (buildings and furnishings) 9%
Carbon in car manufacture 7%
Clothes and personal effects 4%
Food and drink 5%
Holiday flights 6%
Public transport 3%
Private transport 10%
Electricity 12%
Gas, oil and coal 15%

Calculating your personal carbon footprint

Go to www.carbonfootprint.com and click on Calculator. You will be asked for details of your household fuel bills, the different forms of travel you might use (air, car, motorbike, buses and trains) and secondary information about how you shop and recycle. The online calculator will then work out how many tonnes of carbon you produce annually. Alternatively, go to www.direct.gov.uk/actonco2.

Offsetting your carbon footprint

It is important that we all reduce our carbon emissions and throughout this book you'll find ways to do just that. But, being realistic, we aren't going to be able to cut them completely so there are ways you can offset them – in much the same way as businesses use the Emissions Trading attached to the Kyoto Protocol to offset theirs.

When you have calculated your personal carbon footprint, click on the link and you will be offered emission reduction projects you can buy into that will counteract your emissions and go towards making a greener world. These include:

- Tree planting in the UK and Kenya. Tree planting is the best way of taking carbon dioxide out of the atmosphere (sequestration). It will also help protect the land from soil erosion. If you choose to buy in the UK, you will be able to specify which county you want to have them planted in.
- Clean Energy Fund – alternative and renewable energy projects in South America (hydropower) and Africa (from fossil fuels to agricultural waste).
- Improved energy efficiency projects worldwide (the use of low-wattage light bulbs, etc.).

You can also go to www.co2balance.com and set up an account.

The costs are not huge. For instance, for the average carbon footprint of 9.8 tonnes, it would cost just £73.50 to buy into the Clean Energy Fund, £98.00 to have 14 trees planted in Kenya or £164.50 to have the same number of trees planted in the UK.

You can also choose to offset particular parts of it. For instance, unless you get rid of your car completely (not very likely for most people), even if you reduce the amount you use it you are still going to do some mileage a year. You can offset the carbon emissions in the same way as for your whole footprint. And you can offset your carbon footprint when you buy air travel. You may be invited to do so when you purchase your tickets. British Airways was the first to introduce it in 2005 and many others have followed suit (Virgin Airlines sells offsets on board!). It is, of course, a voluntary contribution, calculated at the time of booking. You can also offset them retrospectively: go to www.carbonneutral.com/shop and click on the links. The shop offers a choice of neutral citizen, neutral flights or neutral homes too. It can cost as little as £19.50 to offset the emissions for a small car, for instance, while contributing to reforestation and methane gas collection for electricity and heat. This is just one of the websites offering this service. See also Chapter 10, pages 130–135.

Having encouraged you to offset, I must stress that, as in the corporate world, it's not good enough to just make a payback for what you emit and think that is sufficient. You *must* reduce your emissions as well. The encouraging thing is that, if you do reduce your emissions on a yearly basis and choose to offset them too, you'll see a decrease in the amount it costs you to offset each year – a great incentive!

2

Eco-friendly living

It is important that everyone takes responsibility and does what they can to help. The world is paved with good intentions but you have to act, not just think about it. However, it really isn't that difficult once you've made a conscious decision; it's all about re-education so we get into good habits and, above all, using our common sense.

There is no point, for instance, in driving to a bottle bank just to recycle one bottle; or in setting aside plastic water bottles for recycling but binning all your food cans because you can't be bothered to rinse them out for recycling; or in driving to the farmers' market to buy one bag of fruit.

 Did you know..? The Local Government Association says the UK is 'the dustbin of Europe' because we discard more waste in landfill than any of our fellow countries. Considering we are so small – *and* an island – that is seriously worrying!

Here is a practical guide to the things you need to do. Even if you start by just doing one or two, you'll soon start to find you are thinking in a more eco-friendly way and will actually WANT to put the rest of the suggestions into action – you'll even start to feel guilty if you don't (I know I do!).

Your new life mantra – the 3 Rs

Reduce = do you really need it? If not, don't buy it.

Re-use = don't throw it away; use it for something else.

Recycle = don't bin anything with the recycle symbol on it that can't be re-used. Make sure it goes to the appropriate recycling place – kerbside collection, a recycling bank, the local civic amenity centre or returned to the manufacturer. Suitable food waste and other organic matter should be composted.

The 10 main elements of eco-friendly living

1. Use less gas, electricity and/or oil for heating, lighting and cooking (see pages 126–127).
2. Use less water (see pages 114–115).
3. Don't buy more food and other consumables than you need (see pages 37–39).
4. Re-use and repair rather than replace (see below).
5. Recycle as much waste as possible (see Chapter 6, page 71).
6. Avoid unnecessary packaging (see page 41).
7. Don't use your car unless you have to – walk, cycle or use public transport instead (see pages 129–130).
8. Don't drop litter or fly-tip (see pages 65–68).
9. Look after the countryside (see pages 143–145).
10. Offset your carbon footprint (see pages 20–21).

Repair not replace

Everything we buy has an impact on the planet – the use of natural resources, the effect of manufacture, distribution and disposal. So think about whether you really need something new before you buy it. In this throwaway age, where many commodities have

Did you know..? According to the Local Government Association, 3,000 tonnes of waste ends up in landfill every hour! At that rate, we will run out of landfill space by 2016 – then what? It must not be allowed to happen.

become cheap, we often don't even *think* about getting something repaired. We automatically discard it and buy a new one.

My son, Jim, when he was two and something had broken, used to say (with his little hands on his hips and giving a big sigh): 'Never mind. Have to get a new one!' It quickly became a pet phrase whenever anything went wrong or was damaged. BUT it wasn't long before we realised what an indictment that was on the way we lived so it acted as a timely reminder that we didn't need to buy new all the time. So now we don't; unless it is irreparable, we fix it – and you should see me with the superglue!

Swap shops for everything

When the time comes that you realise you don't need an item any more, whether it be a pop-up toaster or a baby's buggy, you can donate, exchange, lend or sell it through www.reusenetworks. org.uk. It makes great sense!

Another similar idea (apart from actually selling items on eBay or similar sites) is to join Don'tDumpThat. It works on the premise that, although *you* don't want a particular item any more, it's quite likely that someone else will. You simply log on to the website, find the forum nearest to where you live, register, then post online what you have to give away in Offers. There is also a 'wanted' section for those looking for a particular item. You wait for someone to post a message saying they'd like it and then arrange a convenient time for them to come and pick it up. If there isn't a forum anywhere near you, you can let the organisers know that you are interested and they will contact you when one is set up. You can exchange pretty much anything from cameras to caravans but, obviously, nothing illegal or foodstuffs, alcohol, animals or firearms. Check it out at www.dontdumpthat.com.

 Did you know..? In the UK over six million electrical items are thrown away every year and it's thought that over half of them still work or could be repaired (ITGC 2003). What a waste!

Restore or re-use

Before you throw anything away, think if you could make use of it either as it is or as something completely different. There are loads of ideas below to get you thinking but for an amazing list of nationwide companies that re-use and recycle everything (you can get used carpets or even an eco coffin made of recycled cardboard) and to find out how to recycle anything that can be reprocessed, go to www.reuze.co.uk.

Major household items

Bicycles

Millions of us have unwanted bikes in our garages or sheds. Re-cycle (see page 154) is an Essex-based company that is, literally, recycling them to Africa, giving them to people who really need them for transport. If you live too far away for it to make sense to take a bike there, go to www.bikerecycling.org.uk to find a project nearer you. Please note that none of them can come and collect bikes; you have to deliver them.

Brown goods

A broken item of household electrical or electronic equipment may be very easy to repair, so it's worth enquiring rather than just rushing out to buy a new one – *If it ain't totally broke, don't ditch it!* It's also very tempting to buy new music centres, hairdryers and so on just because you like the look of them – BUT next time you just fancy getting the latest gizmo, save your money. Each year we throw away 1.2 million tonnes of household goods, including two million TVs, of which three-quarters end up in landfill. These items produce loads of toxins that contaminate the soil and water. This not only harms wildlife and the countryside, but is also harmful to humans living in the vicinity of the sites. You can't, obviously, re-use broken brown goods but you can recycle them (see page 85).

Computers

Technology moves on and no sooner have you bought a new computer than it's out of date. But you don't have to rush out and buy the latest model and, probably, dump the old one – upgrade the one you have already. You can buy more memory, upgrade the processor and/or upgrade the software. Contact your local computer guru, or there is really helpful information (including pictures) on how to install memory, a graphics card, hard drive or motherboard at www.pchardware.co.uk. If you do need to dump an old computer, see page 88.

Furniture

Apart from the swap shops mentioned before, you can contact the Salvation Army (see page 154), various hospices or local furniture projects run through Shelter (see page 154) or Furniture Re-use Network (see page 152). These organisations give furniture to people who can't afford to buy their own. They will come and collect from you, providing any upholstery meets the required fire regulations. They will not take electrical or electronic items. Alternatively, contact Rag-and-Bone (see page 154)

Oxfam (see page 153) also has several specialist furniture shops.

Curtains

Take to charity shops or visit the Curtain Exchange website (see page 152). It has various branches throughout the country, which you can contact direct. If you feel they are really beyond use – even as children's dressing-up capes, picnic rugs or dustsheets – put them in a fabric recycling bank.

White goods (fridges, freezers, microwaves, etc.)

Because relative costs of new products are down and repairs can be so expensive, many people would rather buy a brand new, shiny item and just dump one that's not working as it should. If you are fortunate enough to find a local repair man (and there are still a few of this endangered species out there), then it makes sense to at least make enquiries and get an estimate. But beware of calling someone out because, even if he says it's irreparable, you will probably be faced with a hefty call-out charge! If, ultimately, you are forced to replace one that's beyond economic repair, buy secondhand or get a reconditioned model – much kinder on the planet and your pocket.

Clothing

Nearly two-thirds of people worldwide use secondhand clothes. Put your (clean!) cast-offs in the bags put through your door by bona fide charities (check for the charity registration number on the bag or accompanying leaflet) or take them to charity shops or clothing banks; this is a great way to recycle and support your favourite charities at the same time. Beware the leaflet drops requesting you to donate your clothes to the third world and to leave them outside your door in a plastic bag on a certain day for collection. They give the false impression that the collection is for charity: but if you read the small print on the leaflet you will see that this is a commercial operation and the clothes will be sold for profit. If in doubt, either give only to charities you have heard of or simply check them out on the web or even in yellow pages before you donate.

Cotton or brushed cotton underpants and teeshirts

- Use as dusters.
- Teeshirts make good school PE bags or storage bags for your best shoes or handbags. Cut off the arms and neck and sew up that end. Make a small cut by the side seam each side of the hemmed end, only through the outer layer of material. Over-sew the cut so it doesn't tear, but only through the top layer, not right through as you need to be able to thread a drawstring round inside the hem – it should look like a small buttonhole at each side. Thread a drawstring (you could use an old long bootlace) through. If there isn't a hard end to the string, fix a safety pin to the end to make the threading easier. Tie the ends of the drawstring together so it can't come out again.

Knitwear

Obviously, good-quality items can go to charity shops but if it's got holes in it or is so misshapen it's not worth donating, try unravelling the wool to re-knit it into something else, perhaps a scarf or a patchwork blanket. Also, your local nursery school might be able to use it for art and craft work.

Shoes

All clean shoes in a good, wearable condition can be taken to charity shops for re-sale. Alternatively, the European Recycling Company, which donates to the Variety Club, has shoe banks all round the country. Make sure they're fixed together in pairs and put in bags.

Socks

We might as well face the fact that few people nowadays have the skill or inclination to darn. But there are still uses for holey socks and for solitary favourite socks that have lost their partner.

- Make a muscle pain reliever. Sew up any holes, fill with raw rice and a few tablespoonfuls of dried lavender. Sew up the end. Heat on High for 2 minutes in a microwave, with a cup of water alongside (to absorb some of the microwaves). Wrap it round or lie it on the painful area and allow the heat to penetrate and soothe.
- Use for polishing shoes, brass, silver or furniture. Slip your hand in, dip in the appropriate cleaner (see pages 49–54) and

away you go. Use one side to apply the cleaner, then turn it over and use the other side for polishing up.

- Again, your local nursery school might want socks for its children to make cuddly snakes or other animals or hand puppets. If they're beyond even this purpose, they can be used for stuffing toys, cushions and so on (as can old tights).
- You could make hand puppets for your own children or grandchildren: buttons for eyes and nose, a strip of felt for a mouth, strands of wool for hair. A step further is a hobby horse. Stuff the foot of the sock with other old socks, chopped-up underpants, tights or other rags. Make a horsey face as above and a couple of ears with card. Fix the leg of the sock over the end of a cane or an old walking stick, and secure firmly with elastic bands or masking tape. Stick some fringed card or sew some wool strands down the leg of the sock, which is now the 'neck' of the horse.

Wedding dresses

If you want to donate or you are looking for bridal wear, Oxfam has more than 10 specialist shops throughout the UK. See page 153 to find a branch near you or for more information.

Food containers

Carrier bags

If you have to use thin plastic bags from supermarkets, at least recycle them as bin liners instead of buying a roll of bin liners – but remember that they will still end up in landfill! Better to buy ethically produced fabric bags from stores or online or use 'bags for life'. Make sure you remember to take them with you to the supermarket; once unpacked, keep them in the car (if you use it for food shopping), by the front door or near your shopping list. If you still leave them behind, ask the supermarket to give you some cardboard boxes – it will have plenty. Take a shopping bag when you do other, non-food shopping too, so you can decline the bags offered to you with your goods and use your own bag instead.

Citrus string bags

Ideally, buy your oranges, lemons and so on loose so there is no excess packaging but, if you do succumb to buying them in string bags, they are great for washing tights and socks so they don't get tangled up with the rest of the wash (check the bags are colour-fast first) and they also make surprisingly good pan scourers – remove any metal, scrunch them up and scrub away!

Drinks cartons

You are not going to want to do this all the time but there are some fun ideas for making toys out of them on the Tetra Pak website at www.tetrapakrecycling.co.uk. Click on Key Issues and then on Download, under the Be Creative heading.

Plastic food containers with lids

Wash out plastic containers with lids, like margarine and ice-cream boxes and small salad tubs, and use them to store foods in the fridge or freezer. Always make sure you label them properly so you know what's in them – particularly in the freezer. It's also important in the fridge because, while you may know what you've put in them, the rest of the family won't and it's a horrible shock if you open the coleslaw tub only to find leftover rice pudding!

Screw-topped jars

Wash thoroughly and keep for filling with home-made jams, chutneys, pickles, etc. (see pages 107–109). They are also good for keeping small loose objects like nails, screws, curtain hooks, etc.

Paper and stationery

Books

Recirculate books to friends, give them to charity shops or see if your hospital League of Friends sells them. Young children's picture books may be welcomed by hospital and medical centre waiting areas. There are book banks at some recycling sites too.

Envelopes

Buy recycled ones when you can. When you receive a letter, don't rip the envelope open but carefully ease the flap apart (if not too stuck fast) or use a paper or table knife to slit the top cleanly. Re-use with recycled sticky labels to re-address, and seal with either glue or sticky tape. The labels can be bought from many of your favourite charities, such as the Woodland Trust (100 labels for £3.99 – www.wt-store.com) and Trees for Life (100 labels for £3.50 – www.treesforlife.org.uk). They are also available from 'green' stores like The Natural Collection (100 labels for £2.95 – www.naturalcollection.com) or Recycled Paper Supplies (50 labels for £2.95 – www.rps.gn.apc.org).

Newspapers

If you have open fires, you can do two things. One is to make firelighters by rolling up sheets of newspaper, starting from one corner. When you have a long tube, fold it in the middle. Hold the middle fold, then keep folding the tube over itself, one side then the other until you have a small block with the ends sticking out. Tuck in one end and leave the other as a taper. Make two or three for a fire. Tuck in between the kindling before you add the other fuel. Light the taper ends.

Alternatively, invest in a newspaper log-maker (I gave my father one over 30 years ago and it's still going strong!). The original ones produce brick-shaped 'logs' but you can now buy cylindrical makers for a more aesthetic finished product. In fact, the cylindrical ones can compress not just newspapers but leaves, twigs and even used teabags! They are available through many of the innovative catalogues that come with your newspaper or check out www.naturalcollection.com or www.greenshop.co.uk.

Other uses are:
- Wrapping food waste (which can then go on the compost heap, see page 111).
- Pet bedding.
- Drawer liners.

Paper

We seem to produce so much waste paper nowadays, but there are many uses you can put it to.
- If your computer printer will allow this (some are too sensitive), keep a stock of A4 paper that has been used on one side only and run it through the printer again on the other side whenever appropriate.
- Use the back for shopping lists or children's drawings.
- Shred and use as small-pet bedding.
- Cross-shred non-glossy paper and mix into compost (see pages 111–112).

Stamps

Many charities use stamps to fundraise. Stamps can be sold on to dealers and collectors, normally by weight but, when rare ones are found, they go for a much higher price. The charity usually receives around £1.50 per kg/2¼ lb for UK stamps and about £12.50 for foreign stamps. Numerous charities offer this facility, from small ones, like specialist disease charities and various horse sanctuaries, to the major ones like RNIB and Help the Aged. I've listed a few here but you can check online to see if your favourite charity uses them. Guide Dogs for the Blind has operated this service for over 30 years but finds the cost of sorting and processing outweighs the benefits (which is why it is important to

follow the steps below before sending off your stamps to your chosen charity).

If you have rare or unusual stamps or stamp albums, Oxfam will be particularly interested (but it will take all of them too) as it has several specialist departments. Contact jawhitaker@ oxfam.org.uk for further details.

To collect stamps for charity:

1. Trim them, leaving about 1 cm/½ in of envelope around each stamp.
2. Separate the UK stamps from the foreign and commemorative ones.
3. Send them to the charity of your choice or to Help the Aged Stamp Appeal (see page 153) or RNIB Stamp Recycling (see page 154).

Other household items

Batteries

So they can be re-used, buy rechargeable household batteries (and a charger) or invest in a battery charger that will also work with ordinary ones. I bought my Green Battery Machine from the Coopers of Stortford catalogue (see page 152).

> **Did you know..?** According to DEFRA, we throw away up to 30,000 tonnes of household batteries every year; nearly all end up in landfill.

You can also buy solar or wind-up chargers for use with batteries, mobile phones and torches from the Green Stationery Company (see page 153). (Wind-up and solar torches are available from camping and hardware shops.)

Candle ends

Use as firelighters in the grate or on the barbecue.

Paint

Paint is always needed by charitable organisations to brighten up shops or other accommodation. If you have a lot, put an advert in your local paper or shop window. Alternatively, contact your favourite local charity – or even your local school – and donate it.

Note: if you are planning to dump solvent-based paint, see page 88.

Plastic flower pots

These are usually made of polypropylene(s) and most councils can't recycle them. Ask at your local garden centre as some are offering take-back schemes for re-use. Look out for biodegradable pots made of coconut shells or coir.

Reading glasses

You can donate your old reading glasses at any opticians in the UK for use by the 300 million people in the developing world who need spectacles to lead a normal life but can't afford them. They will be collected by a company called DX and delivered free to Vision Aid Overseas offices for distribution to countries where they are needed.

Toys

A staggering 40 million toys were discarded last year in the UK, and 13 million of those ended up in the dustbin and then landfill. Every Christmas many lucky children get loads of new toys when they already have cupboards full. The ones they no longer play with, either because they've outgrown them or just because they're bored with them, are left lying around or stored in the loft.

First, make sure your children LOOK AFTER their toys and treat them with the care and respect they deserve. They should learn to put them away when they've finished playing; it's the ones that are left lying around that are in danger of being trodden on and broken. Keep good toys boxed (if they are possible future collectables, they will be worth much more if in their original boxes – and that's less for the recycling bin!). Encourage your children to think about others who don't have toys of their own, who would be extremely happy to have they ones they no longer play with. At Christmas, birthdays or other gift-giving events in your family calendar, persuade them to sort out the unbroken toys they no longer play with. Donate them to any of the following:

- Barnardo's (see page 151) – a charity whose vision and purpose is that the lives of all children and young people should be free from poverty, abuse and discrimination. It no longer has childrens' homes for you to donate to but, for your nearest regional centre, go to the website or contact the head office.
- The children's hospital or ward at your general hospital.
- A children's hospice. For your local one, either look up in yellow pages or contact the Association of Children's Hospices (see page 151).

- Your favourite local charity shop.
- A local playgroup or crèche.
- A toy library. There are over a thousand in the UK and they work just like a book library and provide a wonderful learning/play experience for over 250,000 children. They are also a good social gathering place for parents, carers and children. To find out more about donating or starting a library, contact the National Association of Toy & Leisure Libraries (see page 153).
- Hold a Mums and Tots toy swap party either in your home or arrange it with your local nursery school, toddler group or playgroup. Everyone brings along at least one toy and swaps it for another, so everyone goes home with 'new' toys for their children to enjoy. It's a good excuse for a get-together too!
- Sell online at eBay (www.ebay.co.uk). Alternatively, have a stall at a car boot sale or donate your toys to a jumble sale.

Broken toys

While making broken toys sound again is a good idea in principle, safety issues must be paramount. If you are in any doubt about the safety of a toy, or its suitability for a specific child, then it should not be used.

- One From Two. If you have a toy that's still good but you've lost a particular part, set up a fundraising scheme for your local nursery, playgroup or school. Display an advertising board and the owner of the toy pays 50p to put up an advertisement asking for the part of the toy they need. Someone else may have the same toy but is thinking of throwing it out because it is damaged in some other way. This is ideal for anything from shape-sorters to dolls' house furniture – it even works when a wheel is missing from a favourite car, truck, train or plane.
- Look on eBay for the part you need (www.ebay.co.uk).
- For more complicated repairs, contact the manufacturer or look for a toy hospital. Look in yellow pages or try the following (I haven't given the addresses as they all ask you to email first as there are long waiting lists – just as in human hospitals!): www.toyrepairs.co.uk, www.wellfieldbears.co.uk (for bears and dolls), www.restorationservices.co.uk (for rocking horses, wooden and soft toys and dolls).
- Beyond repair? Instigate a One From Two (see above) to offer parts rather than to seek them.

Wax crayons

Make crayon colouring discs instead of throwing away broken ones. Pull off the paper. Either keep similar colours together or mix them up for a rainbow effect. Put the pieces (break up any that are large) in an even layer in tiny petit four paper cake cases or the larger ordinary ones. Add half a teaspoonful of water to each small case or a teaspoonful to a large one. Arrange in a circle on the microwave turntable and microwave on High in 30-second bursts until just melted. Leave to cool on the turntable then, when set, remove the cases. If melting only a few, put a cup of water in the centre of the turntable to absorb some of the microwaves.

3

Green food shopping

At least a quarter of the UK's carbon dioxide emissions are
attributable to food production and transportation – and that
is only part of the problem. As well as thinking about food miles
and buying locally, we need to consider all that packaging to be
disposed of and being better at buying the right amount of food
for the household to avoid unnecessary waste.

Did you know..? A fruit salad comprising fruits flown in
from around the world contributes more carbon dioxide in air
miles than a family of four produces from cooking in several
months.

Shopping sensibly – save the waste, save the world

Wasted food is not only a disgrace, when so many millions don't
have enough to eat, it is also a terrible waste of money and
resources. With a little careful thought, there is no need for it and
you should feel the impact on your own household bills
immediately – a sure indicator that your new habits will have a
wider, positive impact.

Most of this chapter is just good old-fashioned common sense, so you may be inclined to gloss over some suggestions as obvious; but if you do take the time to put them into practice, you could be surprised at the difference they make. Things become regarded as common sense, after all, because they have benefits for a lot of people.

Take time to plan

Most of us are in a constant rush and would say we don't have time to plan our shopping. But, in fact, you could transform 10 or 15 minutes of dithering in the supermarket aisles into the really useful task of planning your food shopping requirements for the week. You don't have to go into huge detail but just sketch out the main items of your meals before you go shopping.

Many of us have partners or older children who aren't always around for meals. Factor this into your planning as far as possible, so you know how many you are catering for. If you aren't sure, try to cook foods that can be reheated a portion at a time, or that can be frozen if necessary. Don't leave a meal waiting in the oven for hours – it's a waste of fuel and the food will be ruined if it isn't eaten. Keep it covered on the side or, when cold, in the fridge and reheat it when appropriate (see page 102 for reheating leftovers).

Another minute or two that is time well spent is to manage your food supplies. Make sure you have useful essentials in your fridge and store cupboard so you can always prepare a meal even at short notice or 'tart up' the leftovers (see pages 90–102).

Before you go shopping, check to see what you already have so you don't stockpile, with the risk that items will reach their sell-by date before you use them, and then go to waste. You can also use this exercise to give you inspiration on meal planning: if, for example, some cans of red kidney beans have been lurking on the shelf for a while, add a chilli to your meal plans that week.

Do write a shopping list of everything you need. And don't forget to take it with you and refer to it when you are in the store – though you'll find that just writing it down helps you remember what you really need. Most of us use the same store for our grocery shopping, so you can even write your list in roughly the order of the aisles. There are bound to be extras you have forgotten, but this will focus your mind and make sure you buy what you need.

Finally, consider using supermarket internet shopping services, where you order online and have the goods delivered to your home. It saves fuel – one delivery van for groceries for numerous families – and stops impulse buying as you select only what you really need.

Don't shop on an empty stomach. You'll buy much more if you're hungry just because you fancy it. If your tummy's full, you won't be so tempted (that's a good dieting tip too!).

Limit your shopping trips

If you do one main shop each week, you'll soon get into the habit of buying enough but not too much, and you are less likely to buy more than you can eat. You can easily pop out for a few fresh items during the week if you need them.

If you are someone who tends to shop each day, test it out to see if you both spend and waste less. Keep all your food receipts for a normal week, then try the single-shop option and compare the two. Look at the financial aspects as well as how much you have or haven't wasted. If you have a practical demonstration of improvement in front of you, you are more likely to stick to an eco-friendly system.

Buy only what you need

Don't buy more than you need of perishable goods unless you are buying on a special offer to preserve or freeze for later.

Don't buy bigger sizes than you need unless you know you can use them up quickly, otherwise you end up with masses of half-used jars or packets in the fridge or larder that don't get eaten and end up being binned. Larger jars are more economical only if you actually use the contents.

The relatively new phenomenon of 'buy one, get one free' is all well and good, but you may not want that much of a product, particularly if fresh foods end up rotting because you were 'forced' to buy them. That is a false economy. So don't feel *obliged* to have the extra fresh produce if you aren't going to use it or, if you know of someone else in your street who could do with it, then give it away rather than leave it to rot.

If you do take home the extra and you know you can't eat it in good time, freeze or preserve for another time, when possible (see pages 103–109). Even if you put it in the compost, it's better than throwing it in the bin.

Understanding 'best before' and 'use by' dates

If you have time, check the 'best before' and 'use by' dates of foods as you shop and buy the longest shelf lives available. I try to check and select the foods towards the back of the shelves as they are re-stocked from the back and older produce is put at the front for quick sale.

These terms do not mean the same thing. If you understand them properly, you'll not only be safer, but you can also save unnecessary waste.

Best before

'Best before' simply means that the food will be at its best before the date stamped on it. If you use it later, it will be okay but not at its best.

The exception is eggs. The Food Standards Agency recommends that you don't eat eggs after their best before date. However, not so long ago there was no such thing as date stamping and, even now, if you buy eggs from a local farm, they won't have date stamps (though some farmers are good enough to write the collection date on their eggs), so you can always do the old-fashioned fresh test.

The fresh test: put the egg (in its shell) in a glass of cold water. If it floats, it's stale. If it sinks and lies on its side, it's fresh. If it sinks but stays upright, it is less fresh but still safe to eat.

If you do buy from a local farmer who doesn't date his or her eggs, ask when they were laid and don't buy if it was more than two weeks previously.

Use by

'Use by' means you should not eat the food after that date. If you know you are not going to eat food in time and it is freezable, put it in the freezer (see Freezing, pages 103–106).

Sell by

'Sell-by' or 'display until' dates are to help shops control their stock. The only time they'll help you, the consumer, is if they are reduced for quick sale because they are reaching that date. This is where bargains can be had. When you buy such items, always check the 'best before' or 'use by' dates and use accordingly. Alternatively, freeze them (where appropriate) as soon as you get home.

Watch that packaging

If we want our goods in perfect condition then we have to accept that there will be some protective packaging, but we all know that many goods are over-packaged. Polystyrene food trays cannot be recycled easily, nor can shrink-wrap or plastic carrier bags, so make a particular effort to avoid these.

Where possible, buy loose produce rather than pre-packed to avoid such excess packaging.

If you have the choice, buy in glass or cans rather than plastic bottles or coated cardboard cartons. If a milkman still delivers in your area, he will have re-useable glass milk bottles (and will drive an electric vehicle). It may cost a few pence more for the milk but it is convenient and you are helping to sustain a livelihood.

Ban plastic carrier bags

We used always to take our own shopping bags. Now it has been made too easy to pick up a new plastic bag – more likely lots of them – every time we shop. Some stores seem positively to encourage you to use them, while others are better at providing alternatives. But opinions have taken a considerable swing and things are changing. Some shopping precincts, and even small towns, have now banned plastic bags completely, and this good practice is likely to spread quickly once people realise that what may seem at first like a fairly drastic idea can actually work and be popular.

Invest in cloth carrier bags – ideally fair trade ones made from organic materials – or heavy-duty recycled plastic ones and remember to take them with you every time you shop. Plenty of shops now sell re-useable shopping bags at very reasonable prices. The ones that have a flat base and stand up on their own are easiest to use for your main food shopping.

Make a point of refusing extra bags when you buy goods. Other people in the queue will see you using your own bag and may follow your good example.

If you do end up with thin plastic bags, remember to re-use them as bin liners, or recycle them into the bin at your local supermarket.

Locally grown produce

We all take it for granted now that we can get just about any fruit, for instance, we fancy all year round or extraordinary vegetables that, a few years ago, we hadn't even heard of. BUT we don't consider the consequences of that luxury.

I'm not saying we should go back in time and eat only what is grown locally – that would mean no citrus, bananas or other tropical fruit and loads of vegetables would never grace our tables again – but we *should* celebrate what is produced nearer home and buy it when in season. Whether that be enjoying the abundance of fish that is caught off our own shores, eating the fruit and vegetables that are produced locally or meat that is reared on our own farms, we can and should enjoy our own food. It is vital for the environment and our economy and, if you are a foodie, you know it tastes better!

Top steps for buying local food

- Keep abreast of what foods are in season: www.eatthe seasons.co.uk is a good site. Or you could buy my book *A Taste for All Seasons*, published by Foulsham.
- Check the labels on foods for the country of origin and choose UK (and locally grown) where possible.
- Visit farmers' markets (see page 44).
- Buy from farm shops or pick your own. One word of warning: don't go mad – if you end up buying far more than you want or need, that would be wasteful and false economy if you can't freeze or preserve it in some other way (but see pages 103–109 on preserving produce).
- Find local food producers either in yellow pages or on the internet at www.bigbarn.co.uk, www.foodfrombritain.com and www.thefoody.com, to name but three.
- Try to find a local butcher who rears his own meat, or buy it from a farmers' market rather than from the supermarket. If you must buy from the supermarket, then try to buy UK free-range, outdoor reared or, at least, labelled as RSPCA Freedom Food (see Animal Welfare, page 57) and buy from the butcher's counter rather than pre-packed in polystyrene trays and shrink-wrapped. You can also buy seasonally reared, traceable meats direct from farms online. Type 'meat farm shop' into your search engine to find one close to where you live. Alternatively, look in yellow pages.

Food miles

Why buy apples from South Africa in autumn when loads of our own fabulous varieties are ripe, or broccoli from Spain when we have acres of it here at the same time? It doesn't make good food or environmental sense.

Sadly, sometimes we still have a battle to buy British. By some crazy commercial economics, it is cheaper to harvest and transport some food half-way round the world than it is to source it here. Using apples as a good example, some travel as far as 20,000 km to reach our shops – that's nearly 12,500 miles! These food miles have a huge impact on our carbon emissions. But although supermarkets are responding to the push to offer more home-grown varieties when in season, many customers still prefer to buy the imported bright, uniformly green Granny Smiths from France or South Africa or shiny Red Delicious from the USA. If only everyone would learn not to judge the fruit by its skin and to try biting into a crisp, sweet Cox's Orange Pippin or an almost strawberry-flavoured Worcester Pearmain produced in the UK. Producers are trying to fight back and are even using apple-polishing machines to try to make them more alluring to customers! It's a mad world.

There are nutritional implications too. Did you know that broccoli from Spain, for instance, is transported nearly 1,600 km/ 1,000 miles under refrigerated conditions to get to the UK? This has such an impact on nutrients that experts claim that, like peas, the frozen stuff is healthier! The crazy thing is that plenty is produced in the UK anyway. This is true of so many foods from fish, meat and cheese to loads of delicious fruit and vegetables.

The food miles issue is even true of some UK produce, because supermarket chains ferry produce right across the country to a central sorting and packing depot and then transport it again to distribute it to its various stores nationwide. So, even when it is claiming to be local produce, it could still have travelled hundreds of miles. It is also then packed in plastic trays and shrink-wrapped, which all ends up in landfill because we haven't the facilities to recycle it properly. What better reasons for shopping locally at a farmers' market and to take your lovely fresh produce home in your own shopping bags or, at worst, paper ones? However, Waitrose is now sourcing some products locally, within 30 miles of a store. That's progress and, hopefully, other chains will follow suit. But it is still about economics – supply and

demand. If we all demand more local produce, then eventually it will be supplied: but if we continue to be complacent and accept what we're offered, nothing will change.

Farmers' markets

These markets have sprung up all over the country. They are where local growers, farmers and producers get together to sell their own produce direct to the customer. There are strict criteria that have to be met before they can join. Everything they sell must have been grown, reared or produced and processed by the seller.

Shoppers can be sure that they are buying locally produced foods. This usually means within 30 miles (or 50 miles when in large cities or remote towns and villages) from where they were produced. It is recommended that nothing travels more than a maximum of 100 miles. Game must have been shot locally and must be sold by the licence holder. Fish should be sold by the fishermen who caught it. Processed foods must contain at least 10 per cent of local produce. Groups such as the Women's Institute may have stalls, providing that they are the bona fide producers of the goods they are selling and that they meet the other criteria. Look out for the logo opposite, which certifies that the market is a member of FARMA – the National Farmers' Retail & Markets Association (see page 153) – and has been inspected by an independent body to ensure that all the criteria have been met.

Is organic food better for you?

There is much debate as to whether organic food is actually more nutritious. You can argue that an apple is an apple or a steak is a steak, regardless of the nutrients put into it by the soil or the farmer, and I was one of those who thought that. The Food Standards Agency is reviewing its position that there is no evidence to the contrary in the light of a gathering body of evidence that organic food may have health benefits. Early results from a 4-year study by Professor Leifert at Newcastle University have showed that organic foods such as fruit, vegetables and milk contained up to 40 per cent more antioxidants (phytonutrients found in some vitamins and minerals, believed to protect against heart disease, some cancers and degenerative diseases) than their non-organic counterparts.

There can be no doubt, anyway, that consuming foods that have been grown without chemical pesticides and with no dubious additives have to be better for you and the environment and may well taste better too. It's important, though, that you choose seasonal, local and organic when possible, or the carbon emissions produced from the food miles will outweigh any benefits.

Not all organic food is grown to the same standard. All organic food sold has to meet government minimum requirements, but to be sure of '...the highest levels of organic integrity', look for the UK Soil Association's certification symbol (see opposite). The standards

it represents are among the highest in the world (UK5) and cover poultry and meat livestock welfare, crops and nature conservation. On average, UK organic farming uses 26 per cent less energy per tonne of food produced. This is mainly due to not using fertilisers, which are the largest source of carbon emissions in agriculture and the single largest source of nitrous oxide emissions in the world.

Organic fruit and veg boxes

If you enjoy food and are happy to get the best of what is available that week, rather than just buying the same things from your supermarket, or if you don't have time to go to a farmers' market, get a fruit and vegetable box delivered weekly. There are numerous companies offering this service. Key 'organic vegetables boxes' into your search engine, or go to www.ukfoodonline.co.uk or www.alotoforganics.co.uk for more information. The Soil Association also has an online directory at www.soilassociation.org/directory where you can find organic box schemes as well as all kinds of other products and services. Alternatively, look in yellow pages for local suppliers. Some give you the option to tell them of any fruit or vegetables you don't like, so they will substitute an alternative instead, and some offer organic meat and dairy produce too.

Good reasons to eat organic

- No chemical pesticides, which are potentially harmful to us and the environment.
- No dubious additives like hydrogenated fats, monosodium glutamate or aspartame (to name just three of the EU-approved food additives that have been linked to health problems).
- High standards of animal welfare.
- No routine use of antibiotics to speed animal growth (linked with bacterial resistance in people).
- GM-free.
- Better for nature and the environment – there is more natural wildlife on organic farms, fewer carbon dioxide emissions as lower pollution from pesticides and less dangerous waste.
- Potentially healthier – higher levels of essential vitamins and minerals, including immune-boosting antioxidants, have been found in some organic foods.
- Tastes better.
- Known and trusted suppliers.

4

Green household products

We can make value choices when we shop, all of which will have a bearing on the environment. It is important that we are aware that it matters how energy efficient our washing machine is; that the people who grew our coffee beans got a fair price for the commodity; that some cleaning products we use are helping to destroy the planet; and that the fish we are all encouraged to eat may become extinct if we don't support changes to the way in which it is caught. The more we are aware of these and other underlying issues, the more we can actively change what we do right now to make the future better. Here I've covered the basic issues but, if you are interested in discovering more, you could subscribe to *Ethical Consumer* magazine or look at its website – www.ethicalconsumer.org – or check out GreenChoices at www.greenchoices.org.

Another excellent site for buying eco-friendly goods is www.carbonneutral.com/shop. The CarbonNeutral Company was set up to make people more aware of climate change and to provide the wherewithal to do something about it. Apart from offering ways to offset one's carbon footprint, it offers good-quality greener products – everything from energy-saving light bulbs to solar-powered toys. Another of my favourite sites is www.spiritof nature.co.uk.

Choosing household appliances

When you buy a new washing machine, dishwasher, tumble dryer, fridge, freezer, lamp, electric oven or air conditioner, you need to know how much energy it uses. Remember that energy efficiency not only helps the planet, it helps your pocket too. An efficient appliance will use less fuel, so will cost less to run, reduce your household carbon emissions and save water in the case of a washing machine or dishwasher. They are not necessarily more expensive appliances either.

> **Did you know..?** An energy-saving washing machine uses only about a third of the electricity of a less efficient model.

Energy labels

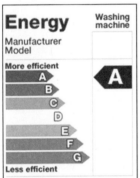

Before you make your final choice, look at the energy labels. There will be the EU energy rating label (see opposite). An A-rated appliance will be the most efficient and will use up to 50 per cent less electricity to run than a G-rated model. All appliances sold by retailers in the EU must display this label.

Energy-efficient models, including gas boilers, hot water tanks and even double glazing, will carry the blue Energy Saving Recommended logo (see below). This is produced by the government-run Energy Saving Trust. You can look on its website for recommended products. Go to www.energysavingtrust.org.uk.

Certification mark

On computer equipment, including game consoles, printers and copiers, etc., you will see the Energy Star (see below). This shows that the machine uses below an agreed amount of energy when in stand-by mode. HOWEVER, for energy conservation, you should turn off all equipment at the mains when not in use (see Chapter 9, page 117).

Eco-friendly household products

Many household cleaners container chlorine bleach, phosphates and other toxic chemicals. These can be damaging to health and also to the environment when they enter the atmosphere and the waterways. You'll see such ingredients as alkyl dimethyl benzylammonium saccharinate in an antibacterial air freshener with a warning HIGHLY INFLAMMABLE beside it, or 'Warning, contains Limonene', a big cross and IRRITANT written under it on a pre-wash stain remover bottle. To quote Dr Gideon Koren, a Canadian paediatrician: 'If you can't pronounce it, should you use it?' We trustingly buy these products because we think they offer us a cleaner, safer home, but we have not the faintest idea what they are doing to our bodies or the environment. There is all sorts of labelling on these products telling us what to do if we touch it, get it in our eyes, swallow it or inhale the fumes. But we pull on our rubber gloves and blithely scrub away. It doesn't make good sense. Some soften the blow by adding such words as 'biodegradable' or 'non-toxic'. Apparently, because these words have no fixed definition, they don't mean much (it's a bit like being told on a label that the biscuits you're buying are low-fat so you think they're good for you, only to discover they have twice as much sugar in them to give them a good texture, so it's a false positive).

The best, much safer, all-round cleaning product you can buy is borax. It is a mineral compound that was discovered over 4,000 years ago and is great as a stain remover for laundry or carpets, as a disinfectant and as a general cleaner. There are also alternative, more environmentally friendly speciality products available from your supermarket or online. You can buy everything you might need from toilet cleaner to eco-friendly non-chlorine bleach. Ecover (www.ecover.com) is a widely known brand. More useful websites are www.soorganic.com or www.ecotopia.co.uk for these and many more eco-friendly products.

You might like to investigate some clever alternatives for your laundry too and put an end to washing detergent and softener. Soap nuts are the nut shells from the soap nut tree. You put about six in a bag in your wash (you can add essential oils for fragrance); the pods last for up the three washes, then you throw them in the compost bin or in with your food waste for recycling. They appear to work better on dark washes, so for heavily soiled and whites you may need an environmentally friendly stain remover too.

Another supposedly amazing invention is a set of Eco Balls. You pop three balls in your machine instead of detergent with a load of washing and that's it. They produce ionised oxygen that penetrates deep into the fibres of the clothes to remove dirt and stains – and they're said to soften clothes in hard water. As they last for a thousand washes and operate on the quick wash programme, you save on energy and water too. They are available through most of the eco-friendly online shops, but for a 30-day trial (or your money back guaranteed), write to the company or visit its website (see page 152) (it doesn't have a shop so don't arrive on its doorstep!).

Home-made household products

If you want to be really green, you can make your own potions with simple everyday products. They worked in Victorian times and, in fact, many branded products are made from the same basic ingredients. You can buy large packets of bicarbonate of soda (baking soda) from chemists and cash-and-carry stores.

General cleaners

Hard floors
Use equal parts of warm water and white vinegar. Add a few drops of natural lemon or peppermint oil for fragrance.

Kettle/coffee machine descaler
Pour in equal parts of water and white vinegar. Bring to the boil. For kettles, just allow to cool, then drain and rinse thoroughly. For a machine, allow the mixture to run through as if you were making the coffee. Leave to cool, drain, then repeat with clean water to flush it through.

Kitchen and bathroom

For taps, surfaces and tiles, put a ¼ of a coffee mug of bicarbonate of soda (baking soda) in a large plastic spray bottle. Add 2 coffee mugfuls of water and shake until dissolved. Pour in ½ a coffee mug of white vinegar and shake again. Use as required.

Loos

Shake bicarbonate of soda (baking soda) all round the pan. Pour round some white vinegar and watch it foam. Scrub well, then leave as long as possible and scrub again before flushing.

Mirrors

Use undiluted white vinegar on a soft cloth (see page 28), then buff up with a soft dry cloth.

Oven cleaner

Mix equal parts of salt and bicarbonate of soda (baking soda) with enough water to form a thick paste. Spread all over the inside of the oven, avoiding any 'stay-clean' areas. Leave for several hours, preferably overnight, then clean off, wash with hot soapy water and then with clean hot water. If the oven is really bad, use a washing soda paste and continue as above.

Shoe polish

Use a little olive oil with just a few drops of lemon juice. Work well into the leather, leave to soak in for 5 minutes, then buff with a soft, dry cloth (see page 28) or brush.

Sink unblocker

Use washing soda crystals. Pour a generous amount (about a coffee mug full) down the sink, pour boiling water over so it dissolves and leave, preferably overnight, then rinse through.

Windows

Use equal parts of warm water and white vinegar and clean with scrunched-up newspaper. Don't clean when the windows are hot or in the sun or they'll streak.

Wood polish

Whisk together 2 tablespoonfuls of olive oil and 1 tablespoonful of lemon juice until blended. Work into wood with a soft cloth (see page 28), then buff up with a clean soft cloth.

Metal cleaners

General scourer
Use dry bicarbonate of soda (baking soda) and a soft cloth (see page 28) or a non-abrasive scourer (see page 29).

Aluminium pans
Boil rhubarb leaves in the pan, then put the leaves in the compost bin and wash the pan well. Or clean with a paste of cream of tartar and water.

Copper pots and pans
Work all over the surface with half a lemon dipped in salt. Rinse, dry and polish with a soft, dry cloth (see page 28).

Gold
Rub with a little white toothpaste (not the gel sort) on a cloth, then polish with a soft, dry cloth (see page 28).

Silver
Make your own dip. Put some milk bottle tops or crumpled aluminium foil in a pan of water with a spoonful each of salt and bicarbonate of soda (baking soda). Bring to the boil and stir well. Drop in the silver, leave until the tarnish has gone, then remove with tongs and polish with a soft, dry cloth (see page 28).

Stainless steel and chrome
Use a cloth dipped in white vinegar. For a sink, put in the plug, pour in a thin layer of vinegar, leave to stand for 5 minutes, then work gently with a non-abrasive scourer (see page 29).

Odour removers

Fridges and microwave ovens
Squeeze the juice of half a lemon into a few tablespoonfuls of water. Add 1 teaspoonful of bicarbonate of soda (baking soda). For fridges, wring out a cloth in the liquid and wipe over all the inner surfaces: for microwaves, put the mixture with the lemon itself in a microwave-safe bowl in the oven and microwave on High for 1 minute or until boiling, then leave in the oven until cold. Wring a cloth out in the liquid and wipe over the inside of the oven.

Hands, chopping boards and utensils
Rub with a wedge of lemon, then wash with detergent-free soap and water.

Rooms

Cut an orange in half and put on a plate, then leave on a surface. Or put some bicarbonate of soda (baking soda) in a small dish and add the coarsely grated zest of any citrus fruit and leave on the side. Or put some ground coffee in a little dish and leave on the side. Or simmer a cinnamon stick and a few cloves in a little water with a slice of orange or lemon; if necessary, pour the steaming contents into an attractive container and take into the room where the smell is prevailing.

Smelly shoes

Use an old pop sock, the cut-off foot of laddered tights or an old sock for each shoe or boot. Put in a large spoonful of bicarbonate of soda (baking soda) and a few drops of eucalyptus oil and tie up to form a pouch. Tuck the pouch into the shoes or boots and leave overnight. Pop the pouches back inside whenever you take the shoes or boots off. You can keep re-using until the scent fades, then remake the pouches with fresh ingredients.

Stain removers

Coffee and tea

Cups or mugs: rub the stain with some bicarbonate of soda (baking soda), then rinse.

Clothing and carpets or upholstery: blot off any excess liquid with kitchen paper (paper towels). For non-colourfast clothing, use cold water only. If colourfast, sponge with a solution of 1 tablespoonful of bicarbonate of soda (baking soda) or washing soda crystals dissolved in 300 ml/½ pt/1¼ cups of cold water. Do not scrub. When the stain is removed, wash the clothes as normal. For carpets or upholstery, do as above, then rinse with a little clean cold water in a wrung-out cloth (try not to make the area too wet). Press a towel over the area to mop up excess, then allow to dry.

Grease spots on washable clothing

Work in liquid soap immediately, then wash as usual. For larger or more persistent marks, soak in a strong solution of washing soda crystals, then wash as usual.

Mould on grouting

Make a paste of lemon juice and salt. Work into the grouting with an old toothbrush. Leave for as long as possible (preferably overnight), then wash off.

Red wine

Washable fabrics: rub the stain well with salt, then lay the soiled material over a bowl. Pour boiling water from a kettle over the stain from quite a height (about 45 cm/18 in), then wash as usual. I don't know where this method came from originally, but my sister-in-law told me about it and it really works.

Carpets and upholstery: get some kitchen paper (paper towel), a bowl of cold water, a cloth and some salt. Blot off the excess wine with kitchen paper, then rinse the cloth in the cold water and remove as much of the wine as possible in a circular motion, but without scrubbing. Add plenty of salt, working it gently into the pile, then leave it to soak up the wine. Brush up most of it and wipe the rest with damp cloth, then repeat. Leave to dry completely (it takes quite a while), then vacuum.

The alternative of putting white wine on red wine does appear to work, if you have some white wine handy.

Teapot stains

Fill the teapot with boiling water, add 1 tablespoonful of lemon juice or vinegar and 1 tablespoonful of bicarbonate of soda (baking soda), stir and leave to fizz, then get cold. If necessary, use a toothbrush to scrub the inside gently, then rinse thoroughly. You can also use an effervescent denture-cleaning tablet dissolved in warm water in the pot and left overnight. Rinse well before use.

Water marks on wood

Work in a little white toothpaste (not the gel sort) using a soft cloth (see page 28). It will take a while, but the mark will go. Buff up with a clean, soft cloth.

Fair food and clothing for a fair price

The Fairtrade Foundation (see page 152) is an independent body offering disadvantaged producers in the developing world a better deal for their produce. Many of the goods sold through the Foundation – like bananas, citrus, mangoes, pineapples, avocados, coffee, tea, cocoa, dried fruit, sugar, spices, rice and some fruit juices – are not even produced here, so make excellent additions to buying home produce. By actively seeking them out (even if it means paying a few pence more), you are making a much-needed difference to people who really need your help. Fairtrade is not just about food products; look out for clothing and accessories too, such as natural cotton and jute products and jewellery. Even high street stores like M&S and Monsoon stock them, but you may have to look carefully! The more we buy, the more products will become available and the cheaper they will become. That's simple economics. Look out for this symbol on produce:

Ethical toys

We can't put the clock back with toys and expect everyone to buy just wooden ones made from sustainable forests or recycled plastic ones. However, we should all take the environment into consideration when we do buy. Wooden toys are a great example of where the traditional is coming back into fashion, so take it a step further and make sure that train or truck, the colouring pencils, rulers and colouring books, you buy have been made ethically. It will be clearly stated. I am not going to go into huge detail here – it's just something to be aware of. Check out www.toys-to-you.co.uk – just one of the websites with a range of ethical kids' playthings.

It's also worth considering charity shops (or look at Oxfam online, see page 153), local newspaper adverts or sites like eBay for excellent quality secondhand toys and games. At least you are re-using the toys and, if you get them through a charity, contributing to those who really need your money at the same time. See also pages 33–35.

Sustainable fishing

Most of us are aware that not only are some fish stocks diminishing due to overfishing but, because of modern fishing by net methods, many undersized or otherwise unwanted fish are also caught. These are simply thrown back but are already dead – senseless destruction and a terrible waste. It's not just fish that suffer: dolphins, seals and other sea mammals are often caught up too. These nets also drag along the ocean floor, damaging the ecological system.

Towing the line

Instead of these lethal nets, the fish can be line caught. By using this more selective method, fisherman can catch the type and size of fish they want, greatly reducing the number of tiddlers or sea mammals destroyed. It also prevents damage to the sea bed. Look for the words 'line-caught' or 'dolphin-friendly' even on canned fish.

Did you know..? According to one prediction, if we carry on fishing at the current rate, global fish and seafood stocks will collapse before 2050.

To address the global problem of overfishing, the Marine Stewardship Council has been set up to promote sustainable fishing practices through an independent certification scheme and helpful eco-label (see below). Fisheries worldwide are encouraged to sign up to the body and are assessed against the MSC standard. MSC does not itself carry out the assessments; they are undertaken by third party certifiers, who independently assess that they are well managed and sustainable. Several main criteria have to be met:

1. Condition of stock: this is about maintaining the stock of the species as a whole. The targeted fish are examined to make certain that there are enough adult young to ensure the stock is sustainable. Historic records of stock levels are also examined.

2. Environmental impact: detailed record-keeping gives an overview of the ocean environment to make sure that other species of fish, marine mammals such as dolphins, and seabirds are not being affected.

3. Fishery management: the procedures and systems are checked to ensure that they are implemented properly to minimise environmental damage and maintain sustainable fish stocks. Fishery management also has to demonstrate an adapting-to-change element in their future management plans.

Successfully assessed fisheries can display the blue tick label, which indicates that they are environmentally friendly. Currently 8 per cent of the world's fisheries are in the programme, although a smaller percentage are actually certified, but the numbers are growing and over 100 major seafood buyers worldwide have pledged to purchase MSC-certified seafood. This is the best indication the consumer has that the fish is from a sustainable source and has been ethically caught.

Animal welfare

I am not going to go into great detail about animal welfare – not because I don't care because I do, and wholeheartedly – but it seems to me, for the purposes of this book, that the issues are obvious. If you care about the environment then you also care about what you eat. Intensive farming means:

- Overcrowding and distress for the animals – a miserable existence.
- Pollution from the volume of excrement.
- An increase of serious diseases like bird flu.
- The growth hormones used get into the food chain with, as yet, unknown consequences.
- The regular use of antibiotics can cause antibiotic-resistant strains of disease.

Therefore, it makes absolute sense to choose meat and poultry raised to higher levels of animal welfare, such as organic and free-range meat and poultry. Try to choose locally farmed meat or, at least, British, not only because it supports our economy but also because it saves on food miles, and UK animal welfare standards are higher than in some countries we import from.

Another excellent idea is to look out for the Freedom Food label (see below). This scheme is dedicated to improving the welfare standards of over a billion farm animals reared for food in the UK, and their experts assess organic and free-range systems as well as well-managed indoor systems that meet the RSPCA's strict welfare standards. Any Freedom Food member (whether that's a farm, haulier, abattoir or other producer or business) displaying this label is subject to annual assessment from a trained Freedom Food assessor. The scheme is also RSPCA-monitored so that, in addition, members are subject to monitoring visits by RSPCA Farm Livestock Officers.

Ethical clothes

I am not naive enough to expect everyone to go completely green when buying clothes. But there are several issues to consider and, if everybody at least thinks about it and buys ethically when the opportunity is there, then that's a great start.

If, for instance, a pair of jeans costs only £3 in a supermarket, consider that it probably came from a sweatshop where workers are exploited. Just one example of what that means was contained in a report from the Environmental Justice Foundation, which has revealed that in China, India, Pakistan, Brazil, Turkey and Uzbekistan more than a million children, some as young as five years old, are working in the cotton producing industry in appalling conditions, working 12-hour days in extreme heat or cold, exposed to spray pesticides that pose a serious threat to their health and enduring verbal, sexual and physical abuse. Does that make it worth paying so little for your jeans? I think not.

Get to know which stores are promoting an ethical conscience by not importing from these sweatshops, by selling environmentally friendly clothes such as fair-trade cotton and jute garments (see pages 54–55), and by offsetting their carbon footprint.

Recycled products

More and more products are being made from recycled materials. I've mentioned some of the major players here but you'll find others dotted throughout the book. Useful sites for everything from gifts to stationery are www.planettrash.co.uk, www.greenerstyle.co.uk and www.simplyfair.co.uk.

Paper

We all need paper products but there are loads of recycled versions available and their price is decreasing because more and more of us are using them. Before you absentmindedly grab the branded product you always buy, stop and look for a recycled version. You'll find toilet rolls, kitchen paper (paper towels), paper tissues and all types of stationery all readily available in high street shops and supermarkets. Brands do vary – some are superb, others not – so don't give up if the first brand you try isn't as good as you'd like. For instance, some people find that recycled toilet paper isn't as soft as some of the more luxurious brands. But, if you look for the quilted ones, they are really very good indeed. An alternative to recycled paper is to buy products from sustainable wood sources, which will be clearly stated on the label (see the logo on page 75).

Plastic

We can't pretend plastic doesn't exist or never buy any. However, when possible buy recycled plastic items. There is a diverse range available such as garden furniture, guttering, compost bins, water butts, pots and seed trays, pipes, desktop accessories, CD and DVD cases, fibre-filled duvets, fleece jackets, hats and gloves, school uniforms, mugs, keyrings, rulers, shoulder bags, home insulation and even the plastic bags and sacks themselves. They will all be labelled as having been made from recycled plastic.

Glass and jewellery

Those wine and beer bottles you chuck out every weekend shouldn't go to waste. You can buy really attractive tumblers, wine glasses and beer mugs as well as candle holders, crockery and even cheeseboards. They are stocked in many homecare shops but you can also buy ranges online.

Everything from recycled fabric to bottle tops and scrap metal is used for jewellery. Check out www.recycledproducts.org.uk or www.thegreenstoreonline.co.uk or key 'recycled glass' or 'recycled jewellery' into your search engine to find a huge variety of mail-order stores.

Disposable nappies

Did you know..? Over 8 million disposable nappies are thrown away each day and most end up in landfill. They take between 200 and 500 years to decompose, so even the first ones ever invented have hardly started yet.

Ecologically minded parents agonise over whether to buy disposable nappies or washable ones. In truth, neither is ideal! Obviously it's a lot easier to throw them away than washing them but, as you'll see from the box above, if we carry on the way we are with the ordinary ones that don't biodegrade, we'll be knee-deep in them very soon. There are also issues about the number of trees felled to produce them. There are two options:

1. Buy biodegradable ones – they will cost a little more than ordinary ones but are much kinder to the environment: try Moltex or Bambo Nature Nappies from www.spiritof nature.co.uk or www.naturebotts.co.uk or other green household shopping sites and major supermarkets.

2. Revert to re-usable nappies but go for organic or fairly traded varieties (check out www.alotoforganics.co.uk, then key in 'nappies'). This is really only an option if you can buy enough so you always wash a machine full or use a machine that will do half loads with less water. I'm not going to suggest washing them all by hand because you'll think I'm completely mad (though it is an option some may consider). Don't tumble dry, except in emergencies, but use an airer or dry outside instead. It's also important to use a nappy soak, otherwise to kill bacteria you would need to wash them at 60°C – which we are discouraged from doing because of the amount of electricity used. The normal chemicals are really harsh for the environment too, so use an eco-friendly one such as Bio D Nappy Fresh. Don't forget to use biodegradable nappy liners.

An alternative to washing them yourself is to pay for a nappy laundering service. It will use much less water and energy than washing at home and is convenient and hygienic. For more details of a service near you, contact the National Association of Nappy Services (see page 153) or your local National Childbirth Trust (NCT) branch.

Feminine hygiene

Tampons and disposable sanitary pads are also a problem for the environment. It takes about 6 months for a tampon to biodegrade, but plastic-backed pantyliners can last indefinitely. One of the biggest problems is that many women still flush them down the loo (about 8 billion a year end up in the sewerage system), with many getting flushed out to sea, causing damage to marine life as well as polluting the sea and the coastline. There is also a concern about dioxin in the conventional products, which is a known carcinogen. It is found in the chlorine bleach that is used in the manufacture of bleached cotton and rayon goods and also in the pesticides used to grow the cotton.

There are solutions. Buy 100 per cent organic cotton or other natural fibre products. They are guaranteed free from chlorine and chemical pesticides and are biodegradable (they may be better for your health too). They are available from major supermarkets or online (see the sites suggested under Disposable Nappies on page 59).

A more radical solution is to buy re-useable products. There are washable cotton pads, natural sponges (from sustainable sources) or soft rubber cups called keepers or moon cups that are worn internally (www.keeper.com or www.mooncup.co.uk) or you can buy them from the the websites listed under Disposable Nappies.

Cosmetics and toiletries

We are all aware that animal testing is still used for some cosmetics and toiletries. There is an EU directive that by 2009 no cosmetics sold in the EU can be tested on animals but there are exceptions, until 2012, where the industry argues that alternative tests are insubstantial. I am not an antivivisection campaigner but I do totally support not making animals suffer needlessly for trivial products manufactured purely for human vanity. If you feel the same, then you need to check labels (and read the wording carefully) or buy online. Try www.greenpeople.co.uk or other shopping sites I've mentioned.

Did you know...? Palm oil is used in a whole range of products from chocolate to cosmetics, bread to biofuel. To grow enough to meet demand, the peat lands and rainforests in South East Asia are being destroyed. This not only has a huge impact on climate change but is threatening species like the orang-utan and Sumatran tiger with extinction. In 2001, many reputable manufacturers signed up to a Roundtable on Sustainable Palm Oil (RSPO) to establish ethical and ecological ways of producing the oil but the devastation has continued. In May 2008 there was a breakthrough. Unilever announced it has set a target to ensure all its palm oil is obtained from sustainable sources by 2015. It is vital that the others follow its example.

5

What a load of rubbish!

The problem with rubbish is that we discard it because we no longer have need of it and, consequently, tend not to care so much about it. Well, that was the case until quite recently when landfill sites started to fill up, the weather went haywire and suddenly we are all much more aware of the need to protect our planet and be much less rubbish orientated.

Did you know..? The Greater London Authority says that up to 60 per cent of the rubbish that ends up in our bins could be recycled – you'll find out more in Chapter 6.

Here is what happens to all the rubbish taken away by your council. There are four ways that rubbish is disposed of:

- **Taken to landfill:** rubbish disposal in modern sites is a bit more complicated than just chucking it in a hole and filling it in. The refuse is compacted in lined, capped cells, then covered to prevent liquid and gases escaping and polluting the surrounding area. A system is then used to draw off the offending liquids and gases as the rubbish rots. The government has put an increasing tax on landfill, which, it is hoped, will put pressure on councils to step up their recycling facilities.

- **Incinerated:** the rubbish is burned in incinerators. This, of course, means carbon dioxide emissions, which we are trying to reduce. In modern incinerators the energy created can be captured and used for electricity (energy from waste – EFW). There are plans for 50 new such incinerators in the UK but, as yet, only a few have actually had the go-ahead. Apart from the cost, when waste is incinerated, about 30 per cent of the matter still remains, which has to go to landfill. Also there are opinions that the emissions from such incinerators could be harmful to humans, so more research is being done. There are also concerns that, if the incinerators prove to be a good way of producing energy, it will encourage more production of waste, not less.

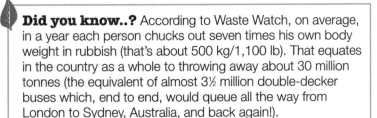

Did you know..? According to Waste Watch, on average, in a year each person chucks out seven times his own body weight in rubbish (that's about 500 kg/1,100 lb). That equates in the country as a whole to throwing away about 30 million tonnes (the equivalent of almost 3½ million double-decker buses which, end to end, would queue all the way from London to Sydney, Australia, and back again!).

- **Recycled household waste:** all the recycling is taken to a Materials Recycling Facility. It is put on a conveyor belt and the different materials sorted. Some facilities are more automated than others. There are different systems that can be used to remove ferrous and non-ferrous metals, paper, glass and plastics, or it can be done manually. The different constituents are then baled before being taken to the appropriate place for reprocessing. This sorting and reprocessing may be in the UK or it may be shipped overseas to other countries that are members of the Organisation for Economic Co-operation and Development (OECD) – even as far as China and India! That's probably not what you expect when you diligently recycle your waste!
- **Composted food and garden waste:** the biodegradable household waste is taken to a centralised composting site. Garden waste from parks and public places, along with farm wastes, sewage sludge and industrial food waste, is taken there

too. Up to three grades of mulch and compost can be made, according to the waste products available.

The most important thing is that there is no glass in it or it would be unsuitable for re-sale. The best quality stuff, with no glass or other contaminants, is used for horticulture; the slightly contaminated (with, maybe, a bit of glass or plastic in it) is used for landscaping and municipal parks and gardens; and the not-so-good mulch, made from solid waste and sewage sludge, is used in land reclamation and to cover and restore full landfill sites.

Fly-tipping

The blot on our landscapes!

According to the Environment Agency, it costs £100–150 million a year to investigate and to remove fly-tipped rubbish. Guess who pays? We do as taxpayers and property owners.

Fly tipping is 'the illegal depositing of any waste on to land' and can be anything from a bag of household waste to fridges, mattresses, tyres, syringes, toxic chemicals – anything that an irresponsible person can't be bothered to take to the civic amenity site ('the dump' to you and me). Apart from being unsightly, it is a danger to the public and to wildlife, it damages the environment and spoils our enjoyment of towns, villages and open countryside. What's more, it is illegal.

Why do people do it?

You may think it odd that people drive out at the dead of night just to dump items on the roadside or in a wood. If they are driving anyway, why not take it to the proper place? The reason is simple – money. Household waste is paid for in council tax but large items are not. Rogue traders will dump anything from rubble to appliances rather than pay to dispose of their waste properly. Some individuals, too, seem to be happy to dump items down the road rather than pay the council to take them away, even though they could easily take them to the proper place for free. They simply can't be bothered to take it a bit out of their way.

Punishment

If you are caught fly-tipping, you can be fined up to £20,000 and/or receive 6 months' imprisonment. A very serious case could go to the Crown Court, where there are much higher penalties –

unlimited fines and up to 2 years' imprisonment (5 years for hazardous waste).

If a vehicle is involved in the tipping, the driver can be prosecuted as well as the owner, if they are different people. The vehicle can also be seized by the police.

What to do if you see someone fly-tipping

1. Don't approach them – they won't be pleased to see you!
2. Don't touch any of the waste as it may contain hazardous materials.
3. Make a note of the date, time and place.
4. Note, too, what the waste looks like and the quantity.
5. Take a note of a description of the vehicle and the registration number, if possible. A description of the people involved would also be helpful.
6. Report the incident as soon as possible:

    In England and Wales: contact the Environment Agency (see page 152) or your local council.

    In Scotland: contact the Scottish Environment Protection Agency (see page 154).

    In Northern Ireland: contact the Department of the Environment's Tidy Northern Ireland Campaign (see page 151).

Keep Britain Tidy

This is a well-known slogan and a well-known campaign, run for over 50 years by the environmental charity ENCAMS (which stands for Environmental Campaigns), but litter is still a big problem in Britain. There seems to be a pervasive 'don't care' attitude and lack of respect for the community. Many people are too lazy or too antisocial to find a bin, and in this take-away, throw-away society it's easier to chuck it than bin it. Litter is hazardous to people and to the environment. It can suffocate, poison, injure and trap wildlife – and humans. It can contaminate and pollute land and water. It can be so unsightly that it affects the community and tourism. It is smelly, dirty and, as most of it isn't biodegradable, unless it is cleared up it will stay indefinitely.

Chewing gum

Around 28 million people in the UK use the stuff and huge amounts of it end up on our streets and stuck to our shoes. Even when it is cleaned off, the marks still remain. In the countryside, it can end up in the stomach of unsuspecting wildlife, which may cause a blockage in the intestines.

> **Did you know..?** A piece of chewing gum costs about 3p to buy but about 10p to remove from the pavement.

The good news is that gum-dropping has fallen by 58 per cent thanks to a recent nationwide campaign and the threat of an £80 on-the-spot fine. However, there are still a lot of chewed lumps lurking. Here is a heartfelt plea to all those (as yet) unreformed gum-chewers. Please, when you've finished chewing, don't spit it out. Wrap it in paper and wait until you find a bin to put it in. If necessary, pocket it and take it home! I vote we follow Singapore and ban it is unless it's issued on prescription.

Dropping litter is a crime!

You can be prosecuted by the police for dropping litter in a public place and can face a fine of up to £2,500 (though, in reality, most people get away with under £100). Some councils have 'litter wardens' who can deal out an on-the-spot fine of £50.

What can you do about litter louts?

ENCAMS says that if you know the person, you can probably ask them – nicely – to pick it up; but, if you don't, it doesn't recommend you confront the perpetrator. You can inform the police or local litter wardens, if you have them, and then it is up to them to proceed and prosecute if they see fit. You could take out a private prosecution but it would be at your expense and you'd have to have a very strong case. So, all you can really do is pick it up yourself!

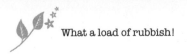

The fast food litter campaign

To try to tackle the dumping of pizza boxes, coke cans, chip (fries) wrappers and burger bags, there's a new 'dirty pigs' campaign aimed at 18 to 24-year-olds. It features an attractive young man and woman growing pig-like features after dropping their fast food rubbish. There is a website (www.dirtypig.org) in conjunction with the poster campaign where you can upload a picture of a mate and 'pig' him or her up with a snout and other piggy accoutrements, then email it to them to make them realise what they look like when they drop litter. A great way to give them the nudge to stop being a litter lout! To get campaign posters of this or other antisocial behaviour attacking campaigns, go to the ENCAMS website (see page 152).

End cigarette ends!

Although I am delighted with the smoking ban, I hate running the gauntlet outside pubs and clubs now because of the wall of smoke and, worse still, all the cigarette butts you wade through on the pavement. I'm obviously not alone because ENCAMS has launched another campaign with the slogan *No butts, stub it, bin it.* In conjunction, there is a range of portable ashtrays that smokers can buy that fit neatly into a handbag or pocket. They can then stub out their cigarette, store it and take it home. Tesco stocks them but they are also available mail order from www.ash can.co.uk, www.stubbi.net, www.buttsandgum.com, www.butts out.co.uk, www.cleanercities.co.uk and www.buttless.co.uk.

Get your council to do more recycling

Nine out of ten people say they would recycle more if it were made easier. If every council took away what was recyclable or provided facilities in every town to deposit the stuff, I think we would all make more of an effort. Even people who say they can't be bothered, once the facilities have been provided, soon get into the habit of separating out the cans and plastic bottles, paper and compostables – it becomes second nature. Why can't the UK be like Germany, which has provided households with different bins for different items for decades? We are so behind, it's a disgrace.

So what can you do about it?

1. Recycle everything that you have been given facilities for.

2. Lobby your council to persuade it to do more. Write a letter on behalf of other residents and get others in your street/block of flats to sign. Send it to the recycling officer at your local council offices (the address will be in the phone book or on its website).

3. Send a copy of the letter, too, to your local councillor so he or she can lobby on your behalf. If you aren't sure who he or she is, just key 'list local councillors' into your search engine and then look up your constituency, or go to your local council website or telephone your council and ask. Alternatively, check in your local library – it will have a list.

4. This is not something to be undertaken lightly, but you could set up your own community recycling scheme. Get neighbours or a whole small community to agree (perhaps talk to your local parish council to get its help). To find out more about what you could do, contact the Community Recycling Network UK (see page 151).

6

Recycling your rubbish

According to DEFRA, on average in 2006–07 the national rate of recycling and composting had risen to 31 per cent. The government targets are at least 40 per cent by 2010, 45 per cent by 2015 and at least 50 per cent by 2020. This is higher than I had thought they were so, while the recycling mentality is going in the right direction, it is clear to me that public awareness must continue to be raised and action accelerated or we will fail to reach these crucial targets and will be swamped in rubbish.

What can be recycled?

If you look carefully, you'll see a symbol on anything that you can recycle. Unfortunately, at the moment it doesn't necessarily mean it can be collected by your refuse collector but you can take a lot of it to recycling banks or your local recycling site (often called the civic amenity centre). See pages 77–88 for more details on what and how to recycle. Obviously, I don't recommend you make numerous trips – that wouldn't be eco-friendly or economical. Get yourself a separate box or bag to put the items in, then make a trip when it's full. You can get a list from your local council website about what and where to recycle.

Here are the symbols to look out for:

General

This symbol means the item can be recycled – note that it does not mean it has been made from recycled material.

Items carrying this symbol (which is a voluntary label) are recyclable *and* contain a percentage of recycled material.

Aluminium

Aluminium carrying this logo is recyclable.

Batteries

This symbol will be used to support the Battery Directive, which is due to become part of UK law in 2008 (see page 86 for more information on recycling batteries).

Electrical and electronic equipment

Electrical and electronic equipment that was made after June 2006 should also display this symbol on the packaging or product. Either send the product to be repaired and re-used or use the bank locator at www.recycle-more.co.uk to find your nearest recycling centre. See also Introducing WEEE on page 85.

Glass
Bank it or put in your recycling box if your refuse collector takes glass.

Ink/toner cartridges
United Kingdom Cartridge Recycling Association: this shows that the cartridges are recyclable.

Steel
Recyclable steel.

Paper
National Association of Paper Merchants: this shows that the paper or cardboard product has been made from a minimum of 75 per cent genuine waste paper and/or board fibre. It should not contain milled waste such as wood fibres.

Paper and board
The RESY System: a German system for reclaiming and recycling used paper and corrugated board shipping containers.

Plastics

There are many different types of plastics with different compositions so unfortunately it isn't as easy as thinking: 'It's plastic, so I'll put it in the recycling box.' Your council will tell you exactly which types it collects – and it may be only plastic bottles. Others will need to be taken to a recycling site or, sadly, binned at the present time. Here are the different symbols:

PETE

1. Polyethylene terepthalate (fizzy drink bottles, oven-ready meal containers)

HDPE

2. High-density polyethylene (milk, fabric conditioner, washing-up liquid bottles)

V

3. PVC (clingfilm [plastic wrap], squash, water and shampoo bottles, some food trays

LDPE

4. Low-density polyethylene (carrier bags, bin liners, waste sacks)

PP

5. Polypropylene (microwaveable containers, margarine tubs)

PS

6. Polystyrene (protective packaging, yoghurt pots, disposable cutlery, foam meat, fish and fruit trays, burger boxes, vending cups, plastic egg cartons)

7. All other resins and multi-materials (the other plastics such as melanine, which is used for plastic crockery)

8. Compostable plastic (this new symbol is on biodegradable plastic packaging and means you can put it in your council organic food waste box or bag)

Wood
FSC Trademark 1996 Forest Stewardship Council AC: the FSC logo indicates that the product contains wood from well-managed forests independently certified in accordance with the rules of the Forest Stewardship Council AC.

Symbols courtesy of WasteOnline.

Kerbside recycling

Most councils collect glass, paper, card, plastic bottles and food and drink cans but, unfortunately, there are inconsistencies according to where you live. My council, for instance, supplies households with one box for paper and cardboard and another for plastic bottles, cans and glass: my mother's council will take paper (but not cardboard), glass, cans and aluminium foil, but not plastic at all, and supplies separate food waste and garden waste bins. Her council will also take batteries, engine oil, textiles and shoes.

Did you know..? 17 trees are saved for every tonne of paper that's recycled (www.recycle-more.co.uk).

All councils are looking at ways to improve their services and are trialling collections of different commodities.

The moral of this story is to read the card your council has given you about what it will and won't collect. If you want its service to cover more materials, tell them; it's the only way we are going to effect change in the near future.

The sad thing is, for most people, if it isn't kerbside collected, they shove it all in the dustbin. Please, if you possibly can, take the time to sort out what can be recycled in your area and take it to your nearest civic amenity and recycling centre or check out www.recycling-guide.org.uk for recycling banks nearest to you. Alternatively, instigate some collections to fundraise: aluminium, for instance, will help fund trees in Africa (see below).

Ten steps to kerbside recycling

1. Check what your council collects and put out only what is accepted (it should have issued you with a list but you can check online on your council's website under Environment or telephone to ask for a list).
2. Always put the items in the right collection box.
3. Always wash out cans, bottles, etc.
4. Remove tops from plastic and glass bottles (metal caps can be recycled too but put separately in the box). Plastic caps can be recycled for charity but not usually with your collection (see page 83).
5. Remove paper labels from metal cans and recycle separately.
6. Flatten all plastic bottles, aluminium cans and cardboard boxes.
7. Some councils will accept broken glass if in a thick envelope and clearly labelled (so the collector doesn't get injured). If not, take it to the recycling centre or bottle bank.
8. Wash foil bottle tops and recycle with other aluminium foil products.
9. Collect other recyclable items in a separate container and take them to a local recycling point (but check online or look up in yellow pages and phone first to see that these items are accepted where you are taking them or you may have a wasted journey).
10. Keep urging your council to collect more. We need to get to a point where every local authority provides facilities for all household recyclable waste.

Did you know..? Glass makes up about 7 per cent of household waste. Every family in the UK, on average, consumes the contents of over 330 glass bottles and jars a year (British Glass).

Flat dwellers

I know there are problems for people living in blocks of flats. Councils often won't supply recycling facilities for you. Ideally, befriend a householder who's prepared to put out your waste with his or her own (my daughter brings hers round to me!). If not, if you can find an outside cupboard or store at your flats, try to persuade the caretaker to allow you to store clean waste (obviously not compostable or other food waste) in there until you have enough to take it to a recycling site yourself. If you are able to do that, make sure you don't abuse the favour. Take it to the recycling site once a week, perhaps when you go shopping if your supermarket provides the facilities.

Aluminium foil and cans

Aluminium can be recycled indefinitely. It takes only 5 per cent of the energy and produces only 5 per cent of the emissions compared with starting from scratch so is fantastically cost-effective and eco-friendly. Some councils will take cans but not foil. Save your cleaned foil containers and foil and take them to your nearest recycling bank. To find yours, go to www.alupro.org.uk. If you are not sure whether some packaging is aluminium, do the scrunch test: if you screw it up in your hand and it bounces back when you stop crushing it, it's not aluminium.

Did you know..? According to Alupro, just one recycled can saves enough energy to run a TV for 3 hours.

Alupro started a campaign in 2007 in conjunction with the charity Ripple Africa to help prevent deforestation in that continent. For every 1 tonne of aluminium recycled, a fruit tree will be planted, so the more that's recycled the better. An even better incentive not to bin it but bank it!

Steel cans

It's not just food and drink cans that are made from steel; nearly all household product cans are, such as deodorants, hairsprays, shoe, furniture and floor polishes, paint and many other DIY containers. Most councils collect them kerbside.

 Did you know..? All steel cans are recyclable, and recycling just seven steel cans saves enough energy to power a 60-watt light bulb for 26 hours – and if it were a low-energy one, that could be as much as 46 hours (www.wasteonline.org.uk).

Food waste

Some councils supply a box for food waste plus a small caddy to collect it in your kitchen. The good thing is you can recycle all the stuff you cannot compost – like cooked meat, bread, bones and cheese so, even if you compost at home (see pages 110–112), you can still make use of the service – once you've given what's suitable to the birds (see pages 138–139). Many people have complained that having food hanging around is smelly and, in the summer, there are maggots and so on, but there are ways to avoid this.

 Did you know..? According to DEFRA, food waste makes up about a quarter of our rubbish by weight.

The top tips for hygiene are:
- Wrap your waste food in newspaper (which is also biodegradable) before putting it in the box.
- Keep liquid to a minimum.
- Store the box in a cool, dry, dark place.
- Keep the lid firmly secured.

What you can put in your food waste bin:
✓ cooked and raw food
✓ fruit and vegetables
✓ meat, cheese and eggshells

✓ bread, pasta and cereal

✓ teabags and coffee grounds

What you must not put in your food waste bin:

✗ garden waste

✗ metal and glass

✗ plastic (even plastic bags)

✗ other household waste

Garden waste

Some councils offer a separate bin for garden waste. If not, never put it in your dustbin; compost what you can and pack the rest in plastic sacks. Telephone your council to arrange collection (it is usually a free service). Alternatively, take it to your local civic amenity and recycling site.

Glass

Bottles and jars are now collected by most councils. If not, bottle banks are in most large supermarket car parks or you can take them to the nearest civic amenity and recycling site. Remember to rinse them out and remove metal lids to recycle separately. Broken drinking glasses may be accepted for collection, if they are wrapped in a thick envelope and clearly labelled; if not, take to the bottle bank.

Do not put in:

✗ toughened glass (e.g. Pyrex)

✗ glass lenses

✗ mirror or plate glass

Paper and cardboard

All paper and cardboard should be recycled. Most councils, at least, collect newspapers and other paper, even if they don't do cardboard. None of it needs to go to landfill, even waxed cardboard cartons (see Tetra Pak cartons, page 85).

You can put in all paper, letters and envelopes (but re-use what you can – see pages 30–31), magazines, greetings cards (but see page 81) and directories. Make sure you shred any important documents, including bank statements, bills, etc., and remove and shred or tear into tiny pieces any names and addresses from labels.

> **Did you know..?** According to Waste Watch, household dustbins are crammed with paper and card – about a fifth of the rubbish. This is equivalent to over 4 kg (about 9 lb) of wastepaper per household in the UK each week.

If your council takes cardboard, make sure you flatten it to save space both for you and when it is collected.

Reducing junk mail

Are you sick of all that unsolicited post? There are two types: that which is addressed to you; and general, unaddressed stuff. The Royal Mail positively encourages the latter because it gets revenue from it!

> **Did you know..?** The Environment Agency says that 550,000 tonnes of junk mail is generated in the UK every year, and it takes six trees to produce 1 tonne of it.

To stop receiving addressed junk mail, contact the Mailing Preference Service (see page 153), where you can register to have your name and address taken off direct mailing lists. But remember that it means you will no longer receive any unsolicited mail, even from companies you might have liked to hear from (such as offers of competitive insurance quotes).

You can opt out of receiving general junk mail delivered by the Royal Mail (about 25 per cent of all unaddressed mail) by emailing or writing to Royal Mail Door to Door Opt Outs (see page 154). Again, though, remember that you won't receive money-off coupons or other items you might have liked.

Free newspapers

If you don't want to receive free newspapers and/or mail, get a sticker from the Stop Junk Mail Campaign (see page 154) to put on your front door. They cost £1.

Christmas and other greetings cards

You can just put them in your recycling box but, to help raise funds to plant trees, donate them. Throughout January, the Woodland Trust arranges collections in high street stores – in 2008 it was WH Smith, Tesco, TK Max and M&S. It's mainly for Christmas cards but you can add any greetings cards during the month. The cards are sorted after collection: mainly white ones are recycled into soft paper like loo rolls and kitchen paper (paper towels); ones with foil and glitter are made into the roll inners, corrugated card and other packaging materials. If the Trust recycles 100 million cards a year, it can raise the money to plant 24,000 trees. For more information, go to www.woodland-trust.org.uk.

Drinks cartons

Juice, milk and soft drink cartons

Tetra Pak cartons – the waxed cardboard ones with foil linings – are recyclable but not many councils offer the facility yet. See page 85 for how to recycle them.

Plastic bottles

Did you know..? It takes 25 of the large, 2 litre plastic drinks bottles to make one fleece jacket (WRAP).

There are more than thirty different types of everyday plastics, some of which are more recyclable than others. Councils don't have the facilities or the finances to recycle them all but most process plastic bottles as there is a huge market for them – that is, for drinks, milk, cooking oil and cleaning, hair, bath and beauty products. Always remember to remove the tops, rinse out the bottles and flatten them before putting them in your recycling box.

Did you know..? Recycling just two bottles saves enough energy to boil about 1 litre/1¾ pints of water.

Polystyrene

This plastic is my biggest bugbear! Everything from the protective packaging in appliance boxes to food cartons and insulated drinks cups are all recyclable but most councils don't have the facilities or finances so it's dumped in landfill and takes up a huge amount of space. The reasons are that it is so light and bulky that it fills up skips and then the transport lorries very quickly, so costs a lot to transport very little, weight for weight. Fish and meat cartons can be contaminated with blood, etc., so become a health hazard and attract vermin before collection and while awaiting processing. Its bulk doesn't break down and the manufacturers say that, if compacted, it's good in landfill because it is stable so doesn't give off toxic fumes. It is, however, still pretty voluminous even when compacted, so that isn't the answer. A new system, called Styromelt has been developed that melts it into dense blocks that can then be recycled for fuel or other products such as garden decking. It is still early days but let's hope it will be widely used in future. The good news is that, as part of the new WEEE regulations (see page 85), manufacturers are obliged to take back packaging (including the dreaded polystyrene) as well as old appliances. So don't put it in your bin; give it back!

I made these points before in Green Food Shopping but they're worth saying again here:

- Avoid buying meat, fish, fruit or vegetables on polystyrene trays. Nearly every supermarket has a butchery and fish counter, where the food will be wrapped, when you've chosen it, in more eco-friendly thin plastic bags or in paper. Buy loose fruit instead of pre-wrapped and *especially* avoid the extra-special, perfectly ripe fruits laid lovingly on specially indented polystyrene trays. Apart from the fact that the goods are seldom as perfect as they are purported to be, you are perfectly capable of selecting loose fruit that is as you want it to be for half the cost!
- Takeaway coffee or tea is a part of life these days but, when you can, take the time to sit down and have it at the shop in a proper china mug. When you do use the disposable ones, crush them up as small as possible before depositing in a waste bin. NEVER dump litter except in a bin. If you regularly go to the coffee shop next to your workplace to buy a coffee to take in with you, treat yourself to a permanent insulated mug with a lid and ask the shop to put your coffee in that instead of the disposable cup.

Fundraise with plastic milk bottle tops

Most councils can't take plastic bottle tops. However, at some plastic bottle banks there is a separate bin for recycling the tops – and you can also recycle milk bottle tops for charity! GHS Recycling (see page 153) will process them into granules and sell them on to make hard plastic toys or more bottle tops. It pays £25 per 500 kg (or pro rata). They need to be clean and completely free from paper or foil inserts or price labels. There are some collection points from Kent to Dorset, outside the M25 and one may be set up in Swindon by the time this is published. Obviously, you need to organise the collection of them and, if necessary, delivery to the company in Portsmouth (you might be able to persuade a local courier to do it for you as it's for charity).

What else can and should be recycled?

CDs, DVDs, video and audio cassettes

Take them to a charity shop or recycling bank; or pack them in a box or sturdy envelope. Weigh the package, write the weight on it and post to The Laundry CD Recycling (see page 153).

Clothing and curtains

Before you throw any fabric article in the bin, stop and think. You can put all items in clothing banks where they will be sorted according to their fabric and sold on for recycling. Trousers, skirts and so on are sold to the 'flocking' industry to be shredded for use as insulation for cars, roofing felt, panel linings, furniture padding – even loudspeaker cones. All wool garments are sold to wool recycling firms, which make it into yarn or fabric again. Cotton and silk are graded, then sold for making cleaning cloths or paper products. Oxfam sends unsaleable clothing and other textiles to its recycling plant, Wastesaver, in Huddersfield (but it prefers to have good clothing as it can get more money for the charity from these) and the Salvation Army operates textile banks too. For more information go to www.satradingco.org.

Foreign and outdated currency

Many charities can benefit from foreign coins and notes you no longer want. They can also use currency that is no longer legal tender, including old British money. Take it to a local charity shop or check out your favourite charity online to find if it uses it.

Ink/toner cartridges

There are recycling bins at most computer outlets such as PC World, or you can contact www.recyclingappeal.com/scope or telephone 08451 302010 to request freepost envelopes to send off your old ones. When you need new ones, instead of buying them from your normal shop, try using recycled ones produced to raise money for charities such as Scope from www.cartridges4causes.co.uk. Other charities also offer this facility.

Mobile phones

These are technically hazardous waste (see page 88) so they must be disposed of properly. But there are also very useful ways to recycle them. If you have a good-quality phone, you can trade it in for another model or sell it back for recycling. Go to www.recycling.tiscali.co.uk to see what your phone is worth. If it is really old and not worth anything, you can order a recycling pack and post it back for free.

There are many other charity recycling schemes; just type 'recycle fundraise' into your search engine and you'll find several to choose from, including Scope. Alternatively, they can go to Oxfam. If you have just one phone, take it to your local shop: if you have ten or more phones, contact the Oxfam Bring Bring Scheme (see page 154) to arrange a free courier collection.

Plastic bags

Most supermarkets now offer a recycling facility, so put them all in one of the bags and take them there. Better still, don't use them in the first place.

 Did you know..? According to Waste Watch, every year an estimated 17.5 billion plastic bags are given away by supermarkets. This is nearly 300 for every person in the UK.

Shoes

Too worn to be donated to charity? Take them, tied or bagged in pairs, to a European Recycling shoe bank. At the moment they are sorted according to their condition, sent to developing countries, restored and re-sold cheaply. Germany is developing a way of re-using the material from badly worn shoes to make sound insulation board.

Tetra Pak cartons

These foil-lined waxed cardboard drink containers are recyclable. One of my biggest concerns is why so many local councils don't collect them kerbside or at a collection point. Other European countries, in general, recycle at least 30 per cent; in Germany, it's nearly 70 per cent. If your local authority doesn't collect them yet, contact it to find out why not and suggest it visits the Tetra Pak website (see page 154). The company offers councils and waste contractors the wherewithal to do it – it is, apparently, a straightforward task to recycle them. In the meantime, check the website for your nearest collection point, or flatten them and post them to Tetra Pak (labels can be downloaded from the website).

Water filters

Brita says all its cartridges are recyclable and, if you send them freepost to the company (see page 151), it will return them to Germany. For other brands, contact the manufacturer; the address or website will be on the packaging.

White and brown goods

White goods are household appliances such as fridges and freezers: brown goods are electrical and electronic products. Each year in the UK we throw out enough electrical goods to fill the new Wembley Stadium six times (www.recycle-more.co.uk)! This is an appalling indictment of the throwaway mentality and it must stop or we'll destroy the environment.

Introducing WEEE

The EC has drawn up a set of Waste Electrical and Electronic Equipment regulations (WEEE). This means that manufacturers and importers of goods now have to join a Producer Compliance Scheme. Distributers (e.g. retailers) must provide facilities for consumers to return old equipment free of charge. Businesses or householders ('end users') do not have to pay for the disposal of the goods – the producers have to fund the collection, treatment and recycling of them. Yes, of course, it means we will pay for it in future in the cost of our goods, but at least there is no reason to fly-tip (see pages 65–66) that old fridge or chuck the portable TV in the bin – you can return them, including packaging, so they can be recycled.

Unfortunately, householders are not under any obligation to comply with the regulations – but they really should. If you are buying a new large item, such as a washing machine, make sure you arrange that, when it's delivered, the manufacturer will take away your old one. For more information and to find your nearest civic amenity and recycling site, go to www.recycle-more.co.uk.

Hazardous waste

This is rubbish that contains anything that may be harmful to health or the environment. Items classified in this category make up only about 1 per cent of all household waste but, if disregarded, can cause serious damage. You probably immediately think of toxic liquid chemicals like chlorine bleach or paint stripper but it goes much further than that; solid items like mobile phones, fridges and freezers are also included. I've listed them all here so there can be no confusion.

The main reasons why these items are disposed of separately is that they can contaminate other waste, pollute land and water, cause damage or injury to the waste collector or endanger the public.

Aerosols
They are not in themselves hazardous but may contain residual flammable or toxic substances. Remove all bits of plastic and put the spray cans in your recycling bin along with other cans. Do not pierce the cans.

Asbestos
You need to contact your local council to check where it is safe to take it. Make sure you are properly protected when handling it.

Batteries
There are lead acid wet cell batteries (used in machinery and cars) and dry cell non-rechargeable and rechargeable ones in all shapes and sizes for most household applications. Rechargeable ones are popular for personal stereos, toys and so on and have lifetime of 4–5 years. They, obviously, reduce the number of batteries that are thrown away, but the metal combination is a known human carcinogen so they must be disposed of safely at the end of their life. All household batteries can be recycled and some councils will collect them in your weekly recycling. If not, take them to your local recycling centre or check with the manufacturer or distributor of the goods about recycling them. See also car batteries opposite.

Car products

Petrol, diesel, brake fluid, antifreeze and rust remover are
flammable so need to be stored in a safe place for disposal. Take
them to your local civic amenity and recycling site. Always hand
them to an operator, don't dump them. Alternatively, ask if your
local garage will take them.

Car batteries should be returned to your local garage or taken
to the civic amenity and recycling site. Do not put car batteries in
the dustbin.

Note that engine oil is recyclable (see page 131).

Cooking oil and fat

Only commercial cooking oil can be recycled at the moment.
Never put cooking oil or fat down the drain – even when made
into an emulsion with washing up liquid, it can clog the system
and pollute, as I've said before. Put it in a container and dispose of
it in your rubbish bin. If you have a very small amount, use stale
bread to soak it up (melt hard fat first) and throw it out for the
birds (see also using up leftovers, page 97, and feeding the birds,
pages 138–139).

Did you know..? 1 litre of oil can pollute 1 million litres of
drinking water (Scottish Oil Care Campaign).

Fluorescent lights and energy-saving bulbs

One tube contains enough mercury to contaminate 30,000 litres of
water; they must be disposed of properly for that reason. Take
them to your local civic amenity and recycling site, where they will
be put in separate storage containers to be taken away for recycling.

Fridges and freezers

Older ones will contain greenhouse gases (CFCs and HFCs):
newer ones won't. They are all dangerous, though, because of
being sealed units. If dumped anywhere, a child can climb in, shut
the door and might be unable to get out. When buying a new one,
get the manufacturer to take the old one away; or contact your
local council to arrange collection (it will charge a fee but you can
usually dispose of a few large household items for the same
money); or take it to your local civic amenity and recycling site
but inform the staff there that you have a fridge or freezer. Civic
amenity sites will not take commercial appliances.

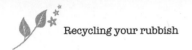

Gas cylinders and fire extinguishers
Compressed gas cylinders usually still have a little gas left in them.
They should be returned to the distributor but can also be taken
to a civic amenity and recycling site. You need to inform the
operator, though, as they are stored in open air cages and then
returned to the manufacturer.

Household chemicals
Cleaning products, bleaches, disinfectants, solvent-based paints,
pesticides, weed killers and fertilizers all come under this category.
Leave them in their original container, clearly labelled. Take them
to a civic amenity and recycling centre and inform the operator.

If you find chemicals and don't know what they are, you will
have to inform the operator and give as many details as you can to
help with the correct disposal.

Note: water-based paints are not hazardous waste and can be
taken to your local recycling site (or see page 32 for re-use).

Medicines
Take them back to the pharmacy. Never put them in your rubbish
or flush them down the loo or sink.

Mobile phones
These are classed as hazardous waste as they contain dangerous
chemicals such as cadmium, which is a carcinogen. They also
contain lead, nickel, mercury or lithium, which are all dangerous
metals so should never just be chucked out. However, there are
ways to recycle them, which I have listed on page 84.

Syringes
Contact your local council to have them taken away and disposed
of. They must be contained separately. If you see syringes in a
public place, do not touch them. Contact your local council,
which will send out an operator to remove them.

TVs and computer monitors
Only those containing cathode rays are considered hazardous
waste. Take them to your local civic amenity and recycling site and
inform the operator.

Tyres
While these are not hazardous, they are banned from landfill. Take
them to your civic amenity and recycling site or your local garage.
They can be recycled.

7

Food - waste not, want not

In the developed world we have access to an abundance of food and it's easy to buy more than we actually need. It's tempting to pick up unusual or tasty-looking items that we hadn't planned to, whether from the farmers' market (my biggest failing!) or from the supermarket shelves. Most people simply don't plan well enough (see Shopping Sensibly – Save the Waste, Save the World, pages 37–41) so buy more than they need and leave the rest festering in the fridge or cupboard and then chuck it out. Well, you can stop the rot now: use up your leftovers, preserve what you can't eat straight away, refresh or revive what has gone a little stale or is tired looking, and compost the edible waste. Not only is that much more environmentally acceptable than just binning everything for landfill, it's also morally right when you think how many people in the world are starving (a cracked record maybe, but true nevertheless). Also, it will save you loads of money and that may be, for some, the biggest incentive of all.

Did you know..? Research by WRAP (Waste and Resources Action Programme) shows that an estimated 6.7 tonnes of food is thrown away in the UK every year, most of which could have been eaten! That's a disgrace when so many people are starving or living so frugally.

A-Z of using up leftovers

I've tried to think of most of the things that get thrown out in an average household. I can't promise it's a complete list but it will give you enough ideas to use many of your tired-looking raw and the last bits of cooked foods that would have been destined for the bin. Once you get into the habit, you'll be using up just about anything rather than slinging it. However, when I've suggested using the oven to make some melba toast, for instance, don't put it on just to process a few slices of bread. Do it only when you have the oven on to cook something else, otherwise it's another false economy (see kitchen tips on page 127).

A

Apples, wrinkled
- Peel, core and slice eating (dessert) or cooking (tart) apples and stew with or without a little honey or sugar. Serve with yoghurt or custard. For sweet apples, add a little tang with a dash of lemon juice.
- Peel, core, slice and fry in a little butter. Serve with pork chops.
- Grate (including the skin) and add to cake mixtures for added moisture, texture and flavour.

B

Baked beans
- Mix with a spoonful of curry paste and a handful of raisins for a curried bean salad (cubes of cheese thrown in are good too).

Bananas, over-ripe
- **Banana bread:** mash 2 or 3 bananas with 100 g/4 oz/½ cup of light brown sugar and 1 teaspoonful of bicarbonate of soda (baking soda) or mix in a food processor. Beat in 50 g/2 oz/¼ cup of softened butter or margarine and then 1 large egg. Mix in 275 g/10 oz/2½ cups of self-raising flour and 1 teaspoonful of mixed (apple pie) spice (at this stage, fold in a handful of raisins, sultanas (golden raisins) or chopped walnuts, if liked). Turn into a greased and lined 900 g/2 lb loaf tin. Bake at 180°C/350°F/gas 4/fan oven 160°C for about 50 minutes until risen, golden and a skewer inserted in the centre comes out clean. Allow to cool slightly, then turn out on to a wire rack to finish cooling. Serve sliced and buttered.
- **Banana smoothie:** blend 1 or 2 very ripe bananas with a glass of ice-cold milk and 1–2 teaspoonfuls of clear honey until

smooth and frothy. If you like, add a peeled, cored apple, or a nectarine or peach or a handful of soft fruit like strawberries. Use half yoghurt and half milk if you prefer. Turn the smoothie into a liquid breakfast by adding a handful of instant oatmeal or porridge oats or a crumbled Weetabix when blending.

Beef (roast)
- **Fajitas or stuffed pitta breads:** cut the beef into strips. Stir-fry some (bell) peppers and onions, cut into strips, for 2–3 minutes until softening. Add the beef and some sliced mushrooms and stir-fry for 1 minute. Add a good pinch of dried chilli flakes and some Worcestershire sauce to taste, then stir-fry for a further 1–2 minutes. Taste and add salt and pepper if necessary. Warm flour tortillas or pitta breads. Spoon the beef mixture on to tortillas and roll up, or split pittas and fill with the mixture.

Biscuits (cookies)
- **Biscuit pie crust:** crush the biscuits (you can use any mixture) and mix with half their weight in melted butter. Press into a shallow flan dish and chill to firm (you'll need about 175 g/ 6 oz of biscuits for an 18–20 cm/7–8 in dish, less for a smaller one). Use as a base for everything from lemon meringue pie to cheesecake.
- **No-bake chocolate biscuit bars:** melt 50 g/2 oz/¼ cup of butter with 1 tablespoonful of golden (light corn) syrup or caster (superfine) sugar and 1 tablespoonful of cocoa (unsweetened chocolate) powder. Stir in 100 g/4 oz of roughly crushed biscuits and a handful of raisins or sultanas (golden raisins). Press into a greased 18 cm/7 in square tin. Allow to cool, then chill until firm. Cut into fingers or squares.
- See also *Scones*.

Bread – sliced
- **Bread and butter pudding:** spread 4 slices with butter and cut into halves. Put 2 or 3 halves in a dish and add a good handful of raisins or sultanas (golden raisins) and 2 tablespoonfuls of sugar. Top with the remaining bread. Whisk 2 eggs in 300 ml/½ pt/1¼ cups of milk. Pour over the bread and leave to soak for at least 15 minutes. Sprinkle with a little more sugar and a dusting of grated nutmeg. Bake at 180°C/350°F/gas 4/fan oven 160°C for about 40 minutes until golden on top and set.

- **Croûtons:** cut the bread into small cubes. Fry in a little hot olive oil, tossing until golden, then drain on kitchen paper (paper towels). Or spread out the cubes on a baking (cookie) sheet and bake 'dry' for about 20 minutes until golden and crisp. Or spread the slices with butter, then cut into cubes and bake in the oven at 190°C/375°F/gas 5/fan oven 170°C for about 20 minutes until golden, tossing once or twice. Store in an airtight container.
- **Crusts from the ends of a loaf:** process into breadcrumbs and store in useable portions in plastic bags in the freezer for use in stuffings, to coat meat or fish (dipped in milk or beaten egg first) or for bread sauce.
- **Melba toast:** cut off the crusts (make these into breadcrumbs as above) and roll the slices flat with a rolling pin. Bake in the oven at 190°C/375°F/gas 5/fan oven 170°C for about 15 minutes until crisp and golden.

Bread – French or ciabatta
- **Bruschetta/crostini:** rub with garlic and fry in olive oil or brush with olive oil and grill (broil) until golden on both sides. Serve with any toppings of your choice. Try sliced tomatoes, fresh torn basil leaves, freshly ground black pepper and a drizzle of olive oil; minced stoned (pitted) olives and canned anchovies; or chicken livers sautéed in butter with chopped fresh sage, a few halved seedless grapes and a little seasoning.

Bread – rolls or bagels
- Cut each horizontally into slices. Place on a baking sheet and bake at 190°C/375°F/gas 5/fan oven 170°C for about 20 minutes until crisp and golden. Allow to cool, then store in an airtight container. Serve instead of crackers.

C

Cake – fruit
- **Ice-cream sandwiches:** cut the cake into even, thin slices. For every two slices, whip a tablespoonful of double (heavy) cream and sweeten to taste with icing (confectioners') sugar. Sprinkle the cake slices with a few drops of brandy, liqueur or orange juice. Sandwich them together in pairs with the whipped cream, then wrap individually in foil and freeze. Unwrap and serve with hot espresso coffee.
- Crumble about 100 g/4 oz and use in place of the Christmas pudding for the Iced Christmas Pudding on page 94.

Cake – plain

- **Good old English trifle:** lay slices in a glass serving dish. Top with canned fruit in natural juice and 2 tablespoonfuls of sherry or liqueur. Cover with canned or freshly made custard, then smother in lightly whipped cream. Sprinkle the top with chopped nuts.
- **Chocolate rum truffles:** melt 25 g/1 oz/2 tablespoonfuls of butter with 2 tablespoonfuls each of golden (light corn) syrup and cocoa (unsweetened chocolate) powder. Stir in 1 tablespoonful of icing (confectioners') sugar and a small handful of chopped raisins. Crumble 100 g/4 oz of plain cake and stir in. Add ½ a teaspoonful of rum essence (extract). Shape with your hands into small balls and roll in extra cocoa powder. Put in tiny paper cases and chill until firm.

Casseroles/stews

- Make into soup. Remove any bones, then purée in a blender or food processor and thin with stock or milk. Add herbs, spices or seasoning as appropriate. Bring to the boil, reduce the heat and simmer for at least 2 minutes.

Chicken

- Use instead of beef for fajitas (see page 91).
- Make a chicken pie (see *Game birds*, pages 95–96).
- **Chicken soup (from the carcass):** break up the carcass and put it in a saucepan with enough water to cover, a chicken stock cube, a bouquet garni (or bay leaf) and a quartered onion (no need to peel). Bring to the boil, reduce the heat, part-cover and simmer very gently for 1 hour. Leave to cool. Strain the stock and return to the pan. Pick off all the bits of chicken from the carcass. Blend 2 or 3 tablespoonfuls of plain (all-purpose) flour with a little milk and 2–3 tablespoonfuls of dried milk powder (non-fat dried milk). Stir into the stock and bring to the boil, stirring, until slightly thickened. Add the chicken meat and season to taste. Heat through for a minute or two. You can throw in chopped cooked leftover vegetables, too.
- **Tropical chicken salad:** chop and mix with some cooked rice, a handful of peas, a diced (bell) pepper and a drained small can of pineapple chunks. Stir in enough mayonnaise to moisten and season to taste. Pile on to lettuce leaves.

Chinese takeaway

- **Chinese pancakes:** brush sheets of filo pastry (paste) with a little oil and fold in halves. Mix together any takeaway you have (chopping up any large pieces of meat or vegetables), including rice. Put a large spoonful towards one edge of the filo sheets in the centre. Fold in the sides and roll up. Either put on a baking (cookie) sheet, brush with a little oil and bake in the oven at 190°C/375°F/gas 5/fan oven 170°C for about 20 minutes until crisp and golden, or deep-fry in hot oil for about 3 minutes until golden and drain on kitchen paper (paper towels).

Christmas pudding

- **Iced Christmas pudding:** separate 3 eggs. Whisk the yolks with 75 g/3 oz/⅓ cup of caster (superfine) sugar until thick and pale. Fold in 175 g/6 oz of crumbled cold Christmas pudding, 200 ml/7 fl oz/scant 1 cup of whipped cream and 2–3 tablespoonfuls of brandy. Whisk the egg whites until stiff and fold in. Turn into a 1.2 litre/2 pt/5 cup pudding basin, cover and freeze. Loosen the edge, turn out and decorate with a sprig of holly. Ideal for New Year!

Cider see Wine

Curry

- **Curry puffs or samosas:** chop up any large pieces of meat or vegetable. Cut ready-rolled sheets of puff pastry (paste) into rounds, using a saucer as a guide. Cut each round in half to form semicircles. Put a spoonful of curry in the centre of each semicircle and brush the edges with beaten egg. Fold up one corner over the filling into the centre, then fold up the other corner to cover the first completely and form a filled triangle. Press the edges together to seal. Either put them on a baking (cookie) sheet, brush with beaten egg and bake at 220°C/425°F/gas 7/fan oven 200°C for about 15 minutes or until puffy and golden, or deep-fry in hot oil for about 3 minutes until puffy and golden and drain on kitchen paper (paper towels).

D

Dried beans, peas and lentils (cooked)

- Throw into any soup, stew or casserole.
- Make a pâté (like hummus). Purée in a blender or food processor with a crushed garlic clove. With the machine running, trickle in sunflower, grapeseed or olive oil to form a creamy paste. Sharpen with lemon juice and season to taste.

- Mash, flavour with garlic, spices such as chilli and cumin and plenty of chopped fresh coriander (cilantro). Shape into small balls. Dip in beaten egg and breadcrumbs and fry until golden.

E

Egg whites
- **Meringues:** whisk the egg whites until stiff. Measure 50 g/ 2 oz/¼ cup of caster (superfine) sugar for every white. Whisk in half the sugar, then fold in the remainder. Spoon in mounds, nests or large rings on a baking (cookie) sheet lined with non-stick baking parchment and dry out in the lowest possible oven for 2–3 hours. Store in an airtight container.

Egg yolks
Store in the fridge covered in cold water so they don't dry out.
- Drain and use to glaze pastry (paste) before cooking.
- Beat into mashed potato or a white sauce to enrich it.
- Whisk with a little milk and stir into soup before serving. Do not allow to boil again or it will curdle.
- **Sandwich filling:** poach in a little water until hard, then mash with mayonnaise.

F

Fish
- **Fish cakes:** you can use just about any fish from salmon to canned tuna. Remove any skin and bones (except canned fish bones, which will give you added calcium). Mash with some cold mashed potato or cooked rice. Add snipped fresh or dried chives, some salt and pepper and a dash of lemon juice. Add a good pinch of hot chilli powder or a chopped fresh chilli, if liked. Mix with a little beaten egg to bind. Shape into cakes, dip in seasoned flour, then shallow-fry in hot oil for 2–3 minutes each side until golden. Drain on kitchen paper (paper towel).

G

Game birds
- Cooked game birds (e.g. pheasant, grouse, partridge), chicken and turkey can be used in a quick game pie: pick off all the meat (you can add a little diced ham, if necessary, to make it go round). Put in a pie dish with sliced mushrooms and some cooked potatoes. Add leftover gravy and/or a can of condensed mushroom soup. Mix well and add 1 tablespoonful of redcurrant jelly or cranberry sauce. Dampen the edge of a dish

and put a strip of puff pastry (paste) or shortcrust pastry (basic pie crust) round the edge. Brush again, then top with pastry. Trim, press together and flute the edge, then brush with beaten egg or cream and make a hole in the centre to let steam escape. Bake at 200°C/400°F/gas 6/fan oven 180°C for about 30 minutes until golden and hot through.

- **Game soup (from the carcasses):** follow the recipe for Chicken Soup (see page 93) but add a beef stock cube and thicken with flour and water instead of milk and don't add the milk powder. Flavour with red wine or port.

H

Ham

- Chop and add to omelettes or use to top jacket potatoes.
- **Potted ham:** mince (grind) or finely chop in a food processor and add a pinch of mustard and mixed (apple pie) spice. Moisten with a little melted butter, then chill until firm. Use as a sandwich filler.

J

Jam (conserve)

- Use the dregs of a jar mixed with a splash of vinegar and soy sauce to taste (add a little garlic powder or crushed garlic, if liked) as a sweet and sour marinade or a baste for pork or chicken.

L

Lamb – roast

- **Make a quick curry:** sauté an onion in a knob of butter or a little oil until softened and lightly golden. Add a diced eating (dessert) apple and a handful of raisins. Stir in curry powder to taste. Cook for 1 minute, stirring. Add 2 tablespoonfuls of flour, then blend in about 250 ml/8 fl oz/1 cup of leftover gravy or some stock. Bring to the boil, stirring. Dice the lamb and throw in, reduce the heat, part-cover and simmer for 15 minutes until tender. Season to taste. Serve spooned over rice and sprinkled with desiccated (shredded) coconut and some chopped fresh coriander (cilantro).

Lasagne or other cooked pasta dishes

- Make into soup (see *Casseroles/stews*).

Lemons or limes
- Squeeze the juice (even when shrivelled or hard on the outside, they will still be juicy inside), store in the fridge in a screw-topped jar or bottle and use as required.

M

Meringues
- **Eton mess:** mash some strawberries and sweeten with icing (confectioners') sugar. Halve or quarter some others. Fold the mashed and pieces of fruit into some whipped cream with some meringues crushed into small pieces (it should have a marbelled effect). Serve within an hour before the meringue goes soft.

Mushrooms
- Use shrivelling mushrooms to make soup: soak in enough water to cover for 1–2 hours, then drain and weigh (you need at least 100 g/4 oz). Sauté with a chopped onion in a knob of butter. Stir in1 tablespoonful of flour, then 250 ml/8 fl oz/1 cup of stock, a good pinch of dried mixed herbs and some seasoning. Bring to the boil, reduce the heat and simmer gently for 20 minutes. Purée in a blender or food processor, then thin with milk or single (light) cream (or a little of each) and reheat but do not boil.

N

Nuts
Refresh stale shelled ones (see page 109) or shell, if necessary.
- Chop and sprinkle on breakfast cereal.
- Mix with cooked rice, a handful of raisins and some cooked or thawed frozen peas, a little seasoning and a splash of French dressing for a nutritional light lunch.

O

Oil – cooking
- Vegetable, seed and nut oils used for deep-frying can be used up to three times provided they are strained well between uses. After that the composition changes and they harden and become saturated fat, which is bad for the arteries. The oil also doesn't heat to a high enough temperature and will not give good results.

Oranges, clementines and other soft citrus

- Halve and squeeze. Store in a sealed container in the fridge for up to 3 days. Drink on its own or topped up with sparkling mineral water (or Champagne!).
- **Caramelised oranges:** remove all the pith and peel (tricky if the fruit is getting a little dry) using a serrated knife. Slice the flesh and remove any pips. Place in a sealable container. Heat 100 g/4 oz/½ cup of granulated or caster (superfine) sugar in a heavy-based pan until melted, stirring occasionally. Boil without stirring until golden. Carefully pour in 150 ml/¼ pt/⅔ cup of boiling water and stir until the caramel dissolves. Pour over the fruit and leave to cool. Cover and chill until ready to serve.

P

Pasta

- **Pasta salad:** mix with tuna, sweetcorn and some mayonnaise or French dressing and seasoning to taste. Add any chopped salad veg such as cucumber, (bell) peppers and/or tomatoes, too, if you like.
- See also *Lasagne*.

Pastry (paste)

- **Cheese straws:** roll out shortcrust pastry (basic pie crust) and sprinkle liberally with strong Cheddar cheese. Dust with cayenne. Fold the pastry in half and roll out again so the cheese is incorporated. Cut into short fingers. Transfer to a baking (cookie) sheet and bake at 200°C/400°F/gas 6/fan oven 180°C for about 15 minutes until crisp and golden.
- **Palmiers:** roll out puff pastry to a thin rectangle on a surface dusted with caster (superfine) sugar. Brush with a little melted butter, then sprinkle liberally with more caster sugar. Fold in the long sides so they meet in the middle, then flip one side over the other. Wrap and chill for 30 minutes. Cut into slices and transfer to a wetted baking (cookie) sheet. Bake at 220°C/425°F/gas 7/fan oven 200°C for 10 minutes, then flip over and cook for a further 3–4 minutes until crisp and golden brown. Cool on a wire rack.

Pears

- **Pear fizz:** peel and core one or two pears (it's all right to use softening ones) and purée in a blender with a pinch of ground cinnamon. Pour into a glass and top up with ginger ale, lemonade or sparkling water.

Pork – roast
- **Pasta sauce:** mince (grind) or finely chop with an onion and some garlic. Cook gently in plenty of olive oil and add some chopped fresh parsley and sage (or use a little dried sage). Season well. Toss into cooked spaghetti or tagliatelle and serve with plenty of grated Parmesan cheese.

R

Rice – cooked
- Make into a salad (see *Chicken* and *Nuts*).
- Throw into any soup for added goodness.
- **Fried rice:** heat a little oil in a frying pan or wok and gently fry a chopped onion or bunch of spring onions (scallions) until soft but not brown. Add the rice and a handful of thawed frozen peas and toss until every grain is glistening. Tilt the pan and pour in a beaten egg. Gradually stir the egg into the rice as it cooks to form shreds of cooked egg. Toss well. Season with a dash of soy sauce and a pinch of Chinese five-spice powder. (You can add chopped cooked chicken or some thawed frozen prawns to make a complete light meal.)

S

Salad (including dressed)
- **Gazpacho (a Spanish cold soup):** soak a slice of bread in cold water. Drain and place in a blender or food processor with the leftover salad. Blend with a crushed garlic clove and a can of chopped tomatoes. Season with a pinch of caster (superfine) sugar and some salt and pepper. Add a little tomato purée (paste), if liked, and a dash of olive oil and lemon juice to taste. Chill and garnish with a little finely chopped cucumber and onion, if liked.

Scones (biscuits)
- **Cobbler:** halve and spread with butter (if you have only a couple left, cut horizontally into 4 slices). For a savoury cobbler, spread with a little wholegrain mustard or sprinkle with a little grated cheese and arrange around a dish of any meat or chicken casserole. For a sweet cobbler, sprinkle with a little demerara sugar and arrange around a dish of stewed or poached fruits. Bake in a moderately hot oven at 190°C/375°F/gas 5/fan oven 170°C for about 40 minutes until the topping is golden and the rest of the food is hot through.

T

Tomatoes, overripe

- **Tomato pasta sauce:** roughly chop at least 4 tomatoes. Sauté a finely chopped onion in a little olive oil. Add a crushed garlic clove, if liked, and the tomatoes. Cover and simmer gently for about 10 minutes, stirring occasionally, until pulpy. Add a pinch of sugar, some salt and pepper and a good handful of fresh chopped basil. Add to cooked pasta, toss and serve with plenty of grated cheese.

Turkey

See *Chicken* and *Game birds*

V

Vegetables

- A mixture of any tired raw or boiled or steamed vegetables can be made into soup. If raw, chop and simmer in some stock with a pinch of dried herbs (either mixed, thyme or oregano) or a bay leaf or bouquet garni for about 15 minutes until really tender. Discard the bay leaf or bouquet garni, if using, then purée with a little cream or a good spoonful of dried milk powder (non-fat dried milk), if liked. Thin with a little milk, if necessary, and season to taste. For cooked vegetables, purée with the stock first, then simmer for 5 minutes and add cream, etc., if liked. Add some grated cheese for added nourishment and flavour.
- **Green beans, cooked:** simply toss with a little finely chopped onion and dress with French dressing for an elegant salad.
- **Greens, cooked:** best for bubble and squeak. Chop and mix with cooked potatoes and season well. Heat a little butter or oil in a heavy-based frying pan, add the mixture and flatten in the pan. Fry fairly gently, pressing down well, for about 10 minutes until crisp and golden underneath. Loosen underneath, put a plate over the top and invert the 'cake' on to the plate. Slide it back into the pan and fry the other side for a further 5–10 minutes. Serve cut into wedges.
- **Peas, cooked:** make minted pea soup. Purée with some stock and a good pinch of dried mint. Season to taste and stir in a little single (light) cream or crème fraîche. Alternatively, throw cooked peas into cooked rice (see *Rice*) for a salad.

- **Potatoes – boiled or steamed:**
  - Cut into bite-sized pieces and toss with a little mayonnaise, thinned first with a dash of sunflower oil and white wine vinegar. Throw in some chopped fresh parsley.
  - Use for bubble and squeak (see Greens above).
  - Sauté in a little oil or a mixture of oil and butter until golden and drain on kitchen paper (paper towels).
- **Potatoes – mashed:** make into Fish Cakes (see page 95) or use for bubble and squeak (see Greens above).
- **Potatoes – roast:** crisp under a hot grill (broiler), turning occasionally. Take care not to burn.
- **Roots (e.g. carrots):** make a quick root cake. You need about 100 g/4 oz of cooked weight. Mash them well. Make an all-in-one sponge mix with 100 g/4 oz each of soft margarine or butter, self-raising flour and soft brown sugar, 1 teaspoonful of baking powder and 2 eggs. Beat together, then fold in 1 teaspoonful of mixed (apple pie) spice and fold the mixture into the mashed roots. Turn into a 450 g/1 lb loaf tin lined with non-stick baking parchment, level the surface and bake in a moderate oven (180°C/350°F/gas 4/fan oven 160°C) for about 40 minutes until risen, golden and the centre springs back when lightly pressed. Allow to cool slightly in the tin, then turn out on to a wire rack to finish cooling. When cold, if liked, spread the top with a little orange or lemon glacé icing (frosting) or butter cream.

Venison
See *Beef*

W

Wine
- Keep corked or in a screw-topped bottle. Use in any dish that calls for wine. A splash will enhance everything from Bolognese sauce to salmon poaching water (white or rosé only for fish). Add to syrup when poaching fruit too.

Y

Yorkshire puddings
- Crisp under a hot grill (broiler), turning once. Serve with sausages or try them with warm syrup, honey or jam as a naughty but nice dessert (or breakfast!).

Top tips for reheating leftovers

You can reheat cooked foods by steaming in a steamer or covered on a plate over a pan of simmering water, by heating in a conventional oven or in a microwave (don't use foil if heating in the microwave). When reheating cooked foods, whether it be a plated meal, a complete dish or an individual item, the following rules apply:

- Cooked food should be reheated only once.
- Always make sure the food is piping hot right through, never just warm.
- To test if a made-up dish is hot through, insert a knife down through the centre, wait 5 seconds and remove. The blade should feel burning hot; if not, reheat for a little longer.
- To test that a microwaved plated meal is hot through, feel the centre of the base of the plate. It should be very hot; if not, reheat a little longer. The food should be reheated with the densest foods towards the outside of the plate (e.g. potatoes round the edge, peas in the centre).
- To make sure foods don't dry out while reheating, they usually need to be covered with a lid or foil for conventional cooking or, if using a microwave oven, use a microwave-safe lid. Covering in sauce or gravy is another way of keeping the food moist. If reheating pastry (paste) dishes or pizzas, this isn't necessary (though a piece of foil laid lightly on top when heating in a conventional oven will prevent over-browning).
- Pastry reheated in a microwave oven will be soft, not crisp.
- Don't use the oven just to reheat a single portion or a plated meal. Use one of the other methods, which will use far less fuel and give a more palatable result.

Storing foods

Make sure you store food correctly at home so it keeps safely and well, and follow any instructions for consuming or storing it once opened. For example, you may be able to keep a jar in the cupboard for a month, but must refrigerate it and use it within a few days once it has been opened. Correct storage will ensure you don't waste food.

Most perishables should be kept in the fridge. If you bought it from the chill cabinet, keep it in the fridge. Bread may keep a bit longer if well wrapped and stored in the fridge, too.

Most fruits are best kept cool, rather than cold. Apples, pears and citrus can be kept in the fruit bowl, provided the room isn't too warm, but a cool larder is usually the best place. If you buy more of these than you can eat quickly, storing them in the fridge or outside in the garage or shed may keep them fresher a bit longer. However for some fruits, like bananas, the fridge is too cold and they go black.

Root vegetables, potatoes and other tubers don't need to be refrigerated; they are best kept in a cool, dark place like a garage or shed. Many people keep them in a vegetable rack in the kitchen but most kitchens are really too hot.

Preserving

There are several ways of preparing and keeping foods for use later. This is particularly important for gluts of home-grown fruit and vegetables or when you've been to a pick-your-own farm. It's also important if you have been tempted by buy-one-get-one-free offers in the supermarket. Here are some general guidelines on how to go about it.

Freezing

Most of us these days have freezers. I've written whole books on the subject, but here are the basic tips to remember when freezing:

Top tips for perfect frozen food

- Freeze only top-quality produce. Foods that are old, damaged or over-ripe will deteriorate quickly and won't improve with freezing.
- Food hygiene is vital. Prepare and freeze raw foods separately from cooked.
- Make sure your hands, your work surfaces and any containers and utensils used are scrupulously clean.
- Cool cooked and blanched foods for freezing to room temperature as quickly as possible before putting them in the freezer. Keep them covered while they cool.
- Fat deteriorates more quickly than lean meat, so remove all excess before freezing raw meat. Blot surfaces of casseroles or stews with kitchen paper (paper towels) to remove any excess fat or oil and drain fried foods on kitchen paper before cooling and freezing.
- Wrap foods properly in biodegradable freezer bags or foil or sealable containers and exclude as much air as possible from the packs. Label and date the packs (you will forget what you've frozen otherwise!). Sealed packs of food, such as meat or fish can be frozen as they are.
- Don't be tempted to freeze foods that specifically say on the label they are not suitable. There will be a good reason for this: either they will spoil (e.g. single (light) cream will curdle on thawing) or they have already been frozen and thawed once, such as fish. (See also pages 105–106.)
- Food can't be frozen indefinitely and some foods will keep longer than others. As a guide:
  Bacon: 2 months
  Bread and cakes: 6 months
  Chicken and other poultry: 12 months
  Fish, oily (raw and smoked): 2 months
  Fish, white (raw and smoked): 3 months
  Fruit: 12 months
  Meat, chops and diced: 8 months
  Meat, joints: 12 months
  Meat, minced (ground): 3 months
  Vegetables: 12 months

- In general, you should never thaw foods and then return them to the freezer without cooking first. You could get food poisoning.
- Don't overload your freezer. Chest models have a clearly marked capacity line and food should not be stored above this. If you have an upright model, don't try to cram in foods so the drawers won't shut properly. If you do, the freezer won't be able to maintain the correct temperature and food will deteriorate. You'll also use far more electricity as the freezer struggles to work properly.
- Keep your freezer free from frost, which will naturally build up inside the cabinet. Use a plastic spatula (not a metal one or you may pierce the casing) to scrape off small amounts around the door or lid and, when the frost is about 5 mm/ ¼ in thick inside, defrost the freezer. If you do not, it can't work properly.

What not to freeze

Most foods can be frozen, though, of course, there is little point in freezing some items – preserved foods, such as pickles, and those with a long shelf life, such as dried beans and raw pasta, for instance. But you should not assume that everything else will freeze successfully.

Previously frozen foods generally should not be refrozen. There are exceptions (such as bread or raw pastry) but, as a rule, thawed raw foods need to be cooked before refreezing. Thawed cooked dishes should not be refrozen – especially meat, fish or poultry ones.

There are also a few foods that cannot be frozen, because the results are unpalatable.

Caviare: becomes watery.

Cottage cheese: becomes watery and chewy.

Cream with less than 40 per cent fat content: curdles when thawed.

Cream cheese with less than 40 per cent fat content: goes grainy and watery.

Custard: only the canned variety will freeze successfully.

Egg-based sauces, such as Hollandaise and Béarnaise: curdles when thawed.

Eggs, uncooked in their shells: will expand and explode.

Eggs, hard-boiled (hard-cooked): will go rubbery.

Garlic: tastes musty once thawed when on its own or used in large quantities for flavouring.

Jam (conserve): tends to become runny – so in a jam sponge, for instance, it will soak into the cake.

Jelly (jello) and aspic: will crack and go cloudy when thawed.

Mayonnaise and mayonnaise-based dressings: will separate or curdle when thawed.

Pasta, plain, completely cooked: becomes unpleasantly soft (undercooked pasta may be frozen, though).

Potatoes, old, boiled: mashed, new or old cut into chips (fries) become watery (par-boiled and tossed in oil, croquette or duchesse freeze well, though).

Salad stuffs, such as cucumber, lettuce, radishes: will go limp and mushy because of their high water content.

Yoghurt: plain varieties will separate when thawed (fruit flavours can be frozen, as can yoghurt in a made-up dish).

Emergency freezing – fruit and vegetables

If you've bought fresh fruit or vegetables that won't be eaten before their use-by date, they can be wrapped and frozen just as they are, without any special preparation (such as blanching), but only for up to a week or two at most.

Ideally, chop or slice them before you freeze. For example, string and slice runner beans, separate cauliflower into florets, shred cabbage, hull strawberries and slice peaches. Place in a plastic bag, foil or a rigid container, seal, label and freeze. Pre-packed fruit and vegetables can be frozen just as they are. When you thaw them they will be a little flabby, so stew fruits, adding sugar to taste, and cook veggies from frozen. Don't leave them in the freezer for longer than a few days or the results will be very disappointing. Don't attempt to freeze salad leaves.

Jams, chutneys and pickles

This is preserving in the old sense of the word. Jams, jellies (clear conserves), chutneys and pickles are all very simple and therapeutic to make. Here are the basic methods to make them:

Jams

As a general rule, use an equal quantity of fruit and sugar. For low-pectin fruit like blackberries, cherries and strawberries, add the finely grated rind and juice of a lemon to every 1.5 kg/3 lb of fruit. Alternatively, you can cheat and add some liquid pectin, according to the directions.

Did you know..? To test for setting point, spoon a little on to a cold saucer and leave in the fridge for 1 minute. If it wrinkles when pressed, the preserve is ready.

1. Prepare the fruit, then place in a preserving pan.
2. Heat gently until the juice runs, then simmer, stirring gently, until pulpy.
3. Stir in the sugar and boil until setting point is reached (see box above).
4. Pot and label.

Jellies

This is a basic, simple method; some recipes are far more complicated. For less tart fruit like blackberries, add the juice of 1 lemon to every 900 g/2 lb of fruit.

1. Prepare the fruit as for Jams above.
2. Place in a preserving pan with 600 ml/1 pt/2½ cups of water to every 900 g/2 lb of fruit.
3. Bring to the boil, reduce the heat and simmer until the fruit is pulpy.
4. Lay a piece of muslin (cheesecloth) or a large, clean, thin rag in a colander, suspended over a large bowl, or use a proper jelly bag over the bowl. Gently tip in the pulp and leave to drip overnight.
5. Measure the juice and allow 450 g/1 lb of sugar to every 600 ml/1 pt/2½ cups of juice.

6   Put in the preserving pan and boil until setting point is reached (see box on page 107).

7   Pot and label.

Marmalades

1. Halve 450g /1 lb of Seville oranges and 1 lemon and squeeze the juice, then strain it into a large pan.

2. Tip the contents of the sieve into a muslin (cheesecloth) bag, tie up and add to the pan.

3. Chop the peel and add it to the pan with 1.25 litres/2 pts/ 5 cups of cold water. Bring to the boil, then simmer for 1½ hours until the peel is soft.

4. Squeeze the bag into the pan to extract the pectin, then discard the bag.

5. Stir in 900 g/2 lb/4 cups of warm preserving sugar until dissolved, then boil rapidly until setting point is reached (see box on page 107).

6. Skim off any scum, pot and label.

Chutneys

For each 1 kg/generous 2 lb of prepared and finely chopped fruit such as apples, plums or tomatoes, or vegetables such as beans, cauliflower and/or marrow, you'll need 2 large onions, finely chopped, 300 ml/½ pt/1¼ cups pickling vinegar (or vinegar and 1 teaspoonful of pickling spices, tied in a muslin (cheesecloth) bag or clean, thin rag), a good handful of dried fruit such as raisins (optional), and salt and pepper (you can also add a good pinch of ground ginger or other spice, like cumin, if you like).

1. Put the onion and half the vinegar in a preserving pan and simmer gently for about 3 minutes until softened.

2. Add the fruit or vegetables, the dried fruit, if using, seasoning and spices, if using.

3. Cook gently, uncovered, stirring occasionally until soft, adding just enough of the rest of the vinegar to stop the mixture from burning.

4. When pulpy, stir in the rest of the vinegar and the sugar. Boil fairly rapidly, stirring occasionally, until thick. Remove the bag of spices, if necessary, pressing it against the side of the pan to extract maximum flavour.

5. Pot and label.

Pickles

Red or white cabbage, shallots or baby onions, eggs, small cucumbers or cornichons or mixed vegetables can all be pickled in vinegar.

1. Prepare the vegetables – shred cabbage, peel onions, cut slightly larger cucumbers into chunks, cut up mixed vegetables (cauliflower, carrots, etc.), shell hard-boiled (hard-cooked) eggs.
2. Sprinkle vegetables well with salt and leave in a colander to drain for 12–24 hours (not necessary for eggs).
3. Rinse thoroughly and pat dry.
4. Pack into pickle jars and cover with cold spiced vinegar. Seal and label the jars. (For sweet spiced vegetables, dissolve sugar to taste in the vinegar before use). For added flavour, add a dried chilli and/or a bay leaf to each jar.

Refresh and revive

Don't throw away biscuits or cereal because they've gone soft or jam that's crystallised – they can be brought back to life. Likewise limp lettuce or other salad leaves can be revived and crisped.

Biscuits (cookies) or crackers

Arrange in a circle in a single layer on a single sheet of kitchen paper (paper towel) on the microwave turntable and microwave on High for 20 seconds. Transfer to a wire rack to cool. Repeat with more biscuits as necessary, then store in an airtight container.

Bread – crusty or French

Brush with a little water and bake in the oven for a few minutes (but only when you are cooking something else – don't waste the fuel on its own) until the crust crisps and the centre is soft. Alternatively, grill (broil) whole until crisp, turning once, but take care not to burn. You can refresh breads in the microwave but only for few seconds otherwise it would harden on cooling. For speed, cut into slices and toast briefly in a toaster or under the grill until hot but not toasted. Eat straight away.

Cornflakes and other breakfast cereal flakes

Spread out in an even layer on the microwave turntable or a large plate (minimum 1 portion, preferably more). Microwave on High for 30 seconds, stir, then continue microwaving in 30 second bursts, if necessary, until the cereal feels crisp, stirring each time. Cool and store in an airtight container.

Honey and jam, crystalline

Remove any metal caps from the jar. Microwave on Medium for 10–30 seconds. Leave to cool before use. Alternatively, stand the jar in a bowl with some boiling water in it and stir occasionally until melted.

Nuts

To refresh raw nuts: cover with boiling water and leave to stand for 3 minutes. Drain and dry on kitchen paper (paper towels). Spread out on a baking (cookie) sheet and crisp in a moderate oven at 180°C/350°F/gas 4/fan oven 160°C for 5 minutes. Don't put the oven on specially – do this when you are already cooking something else.

To refresh roasted nuts: sauté in a little hot olive, sunflower or groundnut (peanut) oil for 1–2 minutes. Drain on kitchen paper (paper towels) and toss with a little salt or a mixture of hot chilli powder, ground cumin and salt to serve as a snack.

Salad leaves (lettuce, rocket, watercress, etc.)

Rinse and shake off excess water. Either put in a polythene box and seal the lid or put in a plastic bag, blow into it and seal the bag. Chill for a few hours. If you've used a bag and blown in to it, rinse the leaves again before use!

Organic waste and composting

If you have any sort of garden at all, it's such a good idea to compost your food waste – it's nature's way of recycling. First you need to get a compost bin or, if you have a large garden, you can just box off a small area with bricks or wood (but a compost bin keeps it all neat and tidy and accelerates the process). Many councils supply bins at a reduced rate. They're made of recycled materials and come in different shapes and sizes to suit the size of your garden and the amount of waste you have. You can telephone the environment department of your local council or look up online at www.recyclenow.com, click on Composting and then use its search engine to see if special offers apply in your area. If not, you can buy them through the website or from any DIY store. You can also buy a small lidded caddy to keep in the kitchen to store compostable waste so you don't have to troop outside with every eggshell or potato peeling (if your council recycles food waste, it will give you a caddy too).

When the waste has been broken down, it provides excellent nutrients for the soil to help you grow healthier flowers, shrubs, fruit and vegetables. It also means there is far less waste going into your dustbin.

Easy steps to composting

1. Put your compost bin on a flat bit of earth that drains well, so water will soak away and worms and other little creatures can get in to help break down the food.

2. Put in a sunny or partially sunny position so the warmth will speed up the composting process.

3. Add your food waste, which can be any of the following:

    ✓ Eggshells
    ✓ Fallen leaves
    ✓ Fruit waste
    ✓ Grass cuttings
    ✓ Plant prunings
    ✓ Shredded paper (not glossy), including kitchen paper (paper towels)
    ✓ Teabags
    ✓ Torn-up cardboard egg boxes
    ✓ Vegetable peelings

Don't add

    ✗ Bread
    ✗ Cans, bottles or plastics
    ✗ Cheese or other dairy products
    ✗ Cooked vegetables
    ✗ Diseased plants
    ✗ Fish and bones
    ✗ Meat or poultry and bones
    ✗ Poo
    ✗ Weeds or seed heads

4. Get the balance right. Make sure you add some torn-up cardboard or scrunched paper along with vegetable matter to keep the compost aerated: if you used all vegetable matter, the compost would be too wet; too much cardboard, dry leaves and grass and the compost would be too dry.

5. Cut up everything you put in the compost small for quicker results.

6. Soft, dark brown compost should be ready in about 9 months at the bottom of the bin. Most bins have a door at the base so you can shovel out the compost that's ready to put on your garden and keep adding at the top.

Creating a wormery

If you don't have much of a garden or only a small amount of food waste, you might like to consider making a wormery, which is a way of composting on a smaller scale.

You start with a small, special bin, similar to a compost bin with drainage holes in it. Add a thick layer of coarse sand or gravel, then top with a layer of a piece of wood or plastic, cut to fit, with holes drilled in it. Top this with a thick layer of compost or leaf mould, add about 100 worms and a pile of chopped food waste, which you put to one side of the bin. Cover it all with a whole wet newspaper. Put on the lid and leave undisturbed for 2 weeks. Don't add more food until the first lot has been processed. Keep the lid on to avoid fruit flies. Add a mixture of waste, just like you would for a compost bin – worms don't like a boring diet!

You can buy complete wormeries or just the worms from www.wormsdirect.co.uk or go to www.wigglywigglers.co.uk.

8

Water for life

Our planet and everything on it needs water to survive, so it is the most important commodity we have. Yet, in the developed world where we have water on tap from a mains supply, we take it for granted. We only ever think about it when drought conditions occur and hosepipe bans are imposed. The problem is, with climate change, we are likely to get longer, hotter summers and wetter winters. These extremes don't mean a sustainable water supply so we have to begin to treat water with the respect – the reverence – it deserves and must have.

 Did you know..? According to the Environment Agency, the average person in the UK uses 150 litres of water a day, 50 litres of which is flushed straight down the loo and 20 litres going down the drain every time they brush their teeth with the tap running.

Each of us can make small changes in our lives to save water. As with recycling, once you start to implement them, they should become second nature.

Easy steps to save water

- Shower instead of taking a bath and set yourself a 3-minute limit by using a timer. You don't need to be under it for any longer. Alternatively, share your bath and make it a shallow one.

- If you do have a bath, use the water for handwashing laundry, or to soak very dirty clothes instead of using the prewash programme in the washing machine.

- Don't leave the tap running when you clean your teeth – it wastes 10 litres per minute.

- When you wash your hands or wet-shave, put the plug in and run a small amount of water into the basin.

- Use a bowl for washing up and don't wash pots, pans and crockery under a running tap.

- Get a save-a-flush bag (free from your water supplier) or put a brick or a plastic bottle filled with sand or small stones in your toilet cistern to reduce the amount of water needed to flush the loo. If buying a new loo, make sure it has a smaller cistern and is dual flush (shorter for 'yellow', longer for 'brown'!).

- Use the washing machine or dishwasher only when you have a full load and always use a water-saving, eco-friendly programme (see page 127).

- Fill a water filter jug or a plastic bottle with water and keep it cool in the fridge rather than running the tap until it's really cold to make a cold drink.

- Mend dripping taps immediately. If you can't, put a container under the drip to collect the water and use it. A drip a second amounts to 13,500 litres (2,953 gallons) a year.

- Water the garden in the evening when the sun is going down, then the water will soak in overnight rather than evaporating in the heat.

- Use a bucket of water to wash your car instead of the hosepipe.

- Collect rainwater in a water butt and use to water the garden.

- Avoid using a hosepipe or sprinkler. A sprinkler, for instance, uses as much water in an hour as a family of four uses in a day. A brown lawn will recover: water resources may not.

- If you have a dehumidifier in your house, use the distilled water for filling the car radiator, to put in the steam iron and to water houseplants.

- Don't cut your grass too short. Longer blades of grass keep the roots shaded so they retain water. Have plenty of ground cover in your flower beds, too, for the same reason.

Water meters

A water meter can be fitted on your property to register the amount of water you actually use and you are then billed accordingly, rather than paying a flat rate in line with the rateable value (RV) of your property. For some this is a much cheaper and fairer way to pay for water. It also makes you more aware of what you use and can help you to consciously save it – for obvious reasons!

According to OFWAT (the water services regulation authority), the average customer can save 5–10 per cent of their bill if they switch to a meter. It does depend, though, on your circumstances: if you live alone or as a couple in a high RV property you will save more than a large family living in a low RV property.

Most homes can have a meter fitted free of charge. There are exceptions, like if the water supply pipe feeds more than one dwelling and it would be costly to create a separate system. In these cases, a charge would be made even though the meter itself would still be free. If it is impossible for one to be fitted, the water company may be willing to offer you an assessed charge, based on other people's metered bills in similar properties.

In some water-scarce areas, household water meters may become compulsory.

You can have a water meter fitted in a rented property if you've lived there for more than 6 months. But you can't switch back if you find it doesn't save you money.

If you want to find out more about whether switching would be right for you, go to www.uswitch.com and click on the water switching service. After answering a few questions you will be told how much, if anything, you could save in a year and given the option to request a meter when appropriate.

What to do if you spot a leak

Leaks mean wasted water, so it's important they are dealt with as soon as possible, whether we're talking about a dripping household tap or a burst water main.

In your home
Make sure you know where your stop cock is so, if a leak occurs in your home, you can turn off the supply and call a plumber.

Outside but within your boundary
You are responsible for mending the leak but you should phone your water company immediately, as it may help you find the leak and carry out the repair, even though you will have to pay for it. Check with your supplier what repair scheme it operates.

In the street
If you see a leak in the water main, phone your water company and report it. Freephone numbers are available on the OFWAT website at www.ofwat.gov.uk or on your water rate bill or look up in your phone book or yellow pages. Don't assume someone else has told them or that they automatically know it's happened.

9

Light, heat, power – take action now

We need to conserve all our resources and look for alternative energy supplies if we are going to save this planet. But it's not just the environment that can benefit, your pocket can too. If you use less energy, you save more money. That's simple economics once again. Here I look at the different types of fuel that can be produced commercially for our use and also what you can use directly in your home.

Alternative renewable energy sources

The EU plans that, by 2020, 20 per cent of its energy will be produced through renewable sources such as solar, wind and tidal power. Also the biggest polluting industries must cut their emissions by 21 per cent compared with their 2005 levels. This will create millions more jobs and should save up to 900 tonnes of carbon dioxide emissions, according to the European Commission. Each member state will have to increase production and use of these types of energy according to set targets. Britain's commitment is to have 15 per cent of energy produced by these and nuclear power by that time.

Nuclear power

The inclusion of nuclear power is a contentious one. At the moment the UK relies on it for about 20 per cent of its total energy, and the government has just backed the building of a new generation of nuclear power plants in the UK. Supporters say that, apart from naturally renewable sources, it is the nearest thing to clean power available as it emits almost no carbon dioxide (though building the power stations to provide the energy will emit huge amounts). It also doesn't rely on hydrocarbons from unstable regimes and the uranium needed to produce it has remained at a stable price for years so it will produce a more reliable fuel, financially, than fossil fuels ever could. They also say that modern nuclear power is economical to produce.

Opposers argue that there is real fear that nuclear power can be used as a terrorist threat. They see no difference between building nuclear power plants for bombs or for electricity and believe that, if we say we are building nuclear reactors to save the planet, so can politically unstable countries. In the past, there have also been some serious accidents at nuclear power stations all over the world (such as in Japan, the USA, the Soviet Union and the UK), in which radiation leaked out, causing death and disease in some instances. These have caused major distrust of the process and the anti-nuclear camp to regard it as dirty and dangerous.

There are also concerns about the storage of radioactive waste. As yet, no firm plans about where to store UK waste have been decided. At the moment it is being stockpiled at Sellafield in Cumbria until a suitable site can be found where it could be put it in sealed deep underground caverns. Perhaps the government should finalise what to do with the increased amount of nuclear waste from the new sites before they are built.

Solar power

As I have said before, I am no scientist. But I will try to explain briefly how solar power works and how solar panels in your home could create some or all of your electricity.

The sun gives out light and heat, and, over the earth's surface, the light can be measured at about 1,020 watts per square metre. About a fifth of this energy can be trapped by photovoltaic (solar) panels. The panels are made up of two types of silicon cell that, when the sun shines on them, create a voltage difference between them. The panels are connected to a lead-acid battery to store the energy, which when connected to an electrical circuit provides an electric current. One panel can create enough energy to charge a 12 volt battery. Usually a number of panels of a similar type are connected in parallel to provide a higher voltage. But, in order to create a current similar to mains electricity, an inverter is attached to change the DC (direct current) from the solar panels to AC (alternating current), which is what we use for power in our homes.

Just for the record, for industrial installations, the sunlight is concentrated to produce heat, which generates the electricity. There are three main ways, but, in a nutshell, it's all done by mirrors!

You can also use solar panels just to heat your water with a compatible boiler. Contact British Gas (see page 151) for more information or a free, no obligation quote.

Wind power

You may have noticed that the UK gets quite a lot of wind; so channelling it as a source of electricity seems a good idea.

The most common way is by setting up wind farms. They consist of a number of wind turbines, each with three wind-facing blades that rotate at 10–30 revolutions per minute. The wind forces the blades to turn, which spins a shaft inside the turbines, connected to a generator that creates the electricity. They create no emissions and can even be placed on land used for something else – livestock grazing, for instance. One drawback is that they are more costly to install and maintain than other sources, so the electricity produced is dearer. However, the more farms that are built, the less the electricity should cost to generate.

Some people are negative for other reasons, particularly if a farm is planned near their home. They say they are unsightly, take up a lot of space, the constant whirring noise is a nuisance, and they cause a slight electromagnetic interference with TV and some communications equipment (but this is supposed to be minimal). Having spent some time near a wind farm in France, I can honestly say I didn't find it either unsightly or noisy.

Unfortunately, most new plans for alternative power sources seem to face strong opposition. For example, there are currently plans for the erection of just one wind turbine in the Weald of Kent and, as is sadly only to be expected, it is causing much controversy. Those in favour are doing what they can to engage with the opponents to persuade them of its ecological wisdom and reassure them that the countryside will not be spoiled or wildlife threatened. They are also writing and giving telephone interviews to the local press to counter the negative articles being published.

Individual wind turbines can be erected for domestic use, too. For more information, key 'domestic wind turbines' into your search engine.

Water power

There are three types – hydro-electric, tidal and wave power. Unless you live in a mill, you are unlikely to use water power as an individual source of energy.

Hydro-electric power: the most common at the moment. Water is stored in a reservoir behind a dam, then released all in one go and the force powers a turbine that creates the electricity. It used to be more popular before we had engines powered by other fuels, when they were cheaper and, so we thought, sustainable. Hydro-electricity produces only about 2 per cent of our electricity and it is unlikely to increase because we haven't enough suitable sites and creating them causes huge disruption to local residents and wildlife and damage to the countryside.

Tidal power: a concept that experts believe could produce over 5 per cent of our electricity in the future and they say the Bristol Channel is one of the best sites in the world for such a system. It works by using the gravitational pull of the moon that creates the rises and falls of the tides to produce energy. Tidal power generators are costly to install but similar schemes in France, Canada, Russia and China have proved to be both productive and economical. There are also environmental concerns because of the disruption to the area and possible pollution.

Wave power: exactly what it says it is – the power of waves is collected and converted into electricity. Experts believe that big storm waves could produce up to as much as 700 watts per metre. Building the pipes or dams to collect the energy could be costly and potentially damaging to the area and to some industries, such as fishing.

Geothermal power

This simply means the earth's heat. Natural hot springs have been used since ancient times for cooking and bathing. The first heating system using natural resources was in the USA in the nineteenth century, and the first power plant, in Italy, at the beginning of the twentieth century.

There are different ways the earth's heat can be tapped: directly – to buildings; or indirectly, via a ground source heat pump that works a bit like a fridge – removing the energy from one source and transferring it to another; or by a power plant that converts the heat to electricity via a steam turbine and generator.

For the home, the most likely option is the ground source heat pump. It could save you hundreds of pounds a year on fuel bills and reduce your carbon footprint by up to 8 tonnes a year (depending on what you are replacing).

An alternative is an air source heat pump. This works on a similar basis to the ground source pump but uses the warmth in the air to provide either an air-to-air system, circulating warm air round your home, or an air-to-water system, heating water to pump round radiators or an underfloor heating system. It needs less space than the ground source pump. For more information on heat pumps go to the Heat Pump Association website (see page 153).

Biomass

Biomass is another word for biofuel. For heating a home, the most usual means is by a biomass boiler – a wood-burning stove to you and me. You can either have a standalone one, which heats the room, with a back boiler for hot water; or a boiler that connects to radiators and a hot water tank. You can use logs, wood chips or wood pellets. They do, of course, produce carbon dioxide but only the same amount as the wood absorbed when it was growing. It is therefore considered to be carbon neutral. The downside compared with other alternative sources is that, unless you have a private supply, you will have to buy the wood. It can still save you money on fuel bills in the long run, though, and reduce your carbon emissions by up to 8 tonnes a year.

More information

To get free help and advice about converting your home to an alternative source of power and to see if you can get a grant, contact the Energy Saving Trust (see page 152).

Ways to save energy in your home

Insulation

There are several ways you can protect your home from heat loss and stop draughts.

> **Did you know..?** According to the Energy Saving Trust, if you have efficient loft insulation, you could save over £100 on your annual fuel bill and nearly 1 tonne of carbon dioxide emissions a year.

Loft insulation

Rolls of insulating material are laid between the joists and then over them in the loft or attic. They act as a blanket, keeping heat in the rooms and preventing it from escaping through the roof. The recommended depth of material is 270 mm; it's worth checking the depth of your existing insulation and, if it's thinner, you should top it up with another layer, says the Energy Saving Trust. You can buy the materials in a DIY store or get it done professionally. Some of it is made from recycled plastic bottles, which has to be good.

If laying insulation yourself:

- Wear a protective mask, gloves and goggles as the fibres can be harmful to your skin and airways.
- Start at the farthest point in the loft (to reduce your contact with the material and to avoid flattening it unnecessarily).
- Don't insulate below the cold water tank.
- Don't compress the insulation under eaves or in corners.
- Lay boards over the insulated joists so you can walk (or crawl) over them to access tanks or to use the loft space for storage.

Pipe and tank insulation

Lagging your pipes and hot water tank can save over 75 per cent of heat loss. Just by giving them a winter coat, you could save 150 kg of carbon dioxide a year. The tank jacket should be 80 mm thick for optimum efficiency and can be bought from a DIY store for less than the price of a couple of cinema tickets. Pipe lagging is also cheap and if your pipes are easily accessible it is easy to install; you may need professional help if they are in awkward places.

Wall insulation

Cavity: most houses built since the First World War have two outer walls with an air gap between them – cavity walls. If this cavity is left empty, although the air helps to prevent some heat loss, a great deal also escapes through them. They can easily be filled with an insulating foam injected from the outside. It has to be professionally done, but takes only a couple of hours for an average three-bedroomed house. You should recoup the cost on fuel bills within 5 years and will save about 750 kg of carbon dioxide emission a year in an average-sized house. Apart from keeping you warm in winter, it will also help prevent condensation and keep the house cool in summer.

Solid: these lose more heat than cavity walls. There are two ways of insulating them. You can add a decorative insulating layer on the outside – a good idea if the outside is in need of serious repair or if the house is extremely cold (in which case, your fuel bills will already be sky high). This layer needs to be 50–100 mm thick. It is, obviously, more expensive but will save you, in an average-sized house, about £300 on fuel bills and up to 2.6 tonnes of carbon dioxide emission a year.

You can also insulate on the inside, using plasterboard lined with insulating material to a total thickness of 90 mm, which will have almost as good an effect as external insulation. Another option is to line your walls with a flexible insulating material, bought, like wallpaper, by the roll. The fuel and carbon dioxide savings are not as high but will still make a significant difference to your bills, to carbon dioxide reduction and to how warm your house feels.

Draught excluders

If you have floorboards, you can prevent draughts by lifting them and laying mineral wool insulation between the joists. A less disruptive method is to inject a silicone sealant in the gaps between the boards and around the skirting boards. Be careful not to block the airbricks that will be below floor level around the walls, which must be allowed to ventilate from the outside or the boards will rot and the house will become damp. All the necessary materials will be available at your local DIY store.

You can use good old-fashioned draught excluders under doors if draughts rush in. These can be removable (people have padded fabric tubes, perhaps made into snakes, sausage dogs, etc. – and what a great way to recycle wool and fabric for the padding!) or you can buy flaps, brushes or strips that attach to the bottom of the doors or strips of insulation that stick round the door frames so they fit more snugly.

Double glazing

This traps air between two panes of glass, creating a barrier to prevent heat escaping and noise and draughts entering. If all the windows in an average three-bedroomed house are double-glazed, it could save up to 750 kg of carbon dioxide emission and about £90 in fuel bills a year. Always look for the energy-saving logo (see page 48) when you buy your windows for the most efficient ones. They are graded A–G like washing machines.

A cheaper alternative is to buy secondary double glazing, which is a layer of glass or clear plastic that is mounted on the inside of the windows.

Funds available to help you

There are several ways you may be able to get some financial help with insulating your home.

Government grants

Homeowners and private tenants on benefits are entitled to a grant for loft or cavity wall insulation under the government's Warm Front Scheme in England, the Warm Deal in Scotland, Home Energy Efficiency in Wales, and the Warm Homes Scheme in Northern Ireland. If you are over 70 years old in England or 80 in Wales, you may be entitled to free insulation. If you privately rent your property you will need permission from your landlord to go ahead. Those in social housing should not apply but contact their landlord. To check if you are eligible, go to www.direct.gov.uk or call Eaga Partnership, the Warm Front Scheme Manager (see page 152) or contact your local Energy Efficiency Advice Centre (see page 152).

Utility supplier and council grants

Some grants may also be available to you through your utilities providers and/or your local council. To see if any are operating in your area, go to the Energy Saving Trust website at www.energy savingtrust.org.uk and click on What Can I Do Today?, then Energy Saving Grants and Offers. Alternatively, phone your local Energy Saving Advice Centre (see page 152).

A better boiler

Many people have gas, oil or electric boilers for central heating and hot water that have been around for years. They will not be energy efficient, emitting loads of carbon dioxide and wasting your money. Look into the possibility of upgrading to a high-efficiency condensing boiler. There are three types:

Combination ('combi') boilers: these heat the house and provide hot water as needed, rather than heating up a tankful. They are the most popular new boilers.

System boilers: these use stored water in a conventional way but the boiler has most of the heating and hot water system components built in, so it takes up less space and is more energy efficient.

Regular condensing boilers: these are for small and average-sized homes where there is a traditional heating and hot water system with a separate hot water tank. These will not be suitable if you have a large home with several bathrooms. They take up more space than the other two types of boiler and need an expansion tank in the loft.

Boiler care

It is important, whatever boiler type you have (even old ones), that you have it serviced once a year by a CORGI-registered engineer for a gas boiler, OFTEC for oil or NICEIC-approved for electric. This will ensure your system works as efficiently as it can. Also, keep the boiler clean and free from dust by wiping the cabinet regularly with a damp cloth. Radiators should also have a rust and limescale prevention agent added, such as Fernox.

Small steps to energy efficiency in your home

Heating
- Turn your heating thermostat down by just 1°C and you will save up to 10 per cent of your fuel bills and reduce carbon emissions.
- Check the temperature of your water; it should not be set above 60°C/140°F.
- Wear sensible clothes – rather than turn up the heating, put on another layer.
- Heat only those rooms you need to, so fit radiator thermostats.
- In winter, keep the house at a constant temperature of about 17–20°C rather than having it on a timer – it costs less to keep the house at a steady warm temperature rather than heating it each time from icy cold and it also prevents pipes freezing at night.
- Draw the curtains at night to keep in the warmth.

Power
- Change to an energy provider that offers green energy and a more cost-effective package. Go to <u>www.uswitch.com/ energy</u> to compare prices.
- Invest in low-energy light bulbs – they use up to 80 per cent less electricity and can last up to ten times as long. Their cost is now coming down dramatically and many mail order stores offer good deals on multi-buys. You can buy them in supermarkets, in DIY and specialist shops and by mail order. If you think there are only the peculiar, tall column affairs that stick out the tops of your lampshades, think again. You can now buy all sorts – even candle bulbs. Look at <u>www.the lightbulb.co.uk</u> to see the whole range that is available.
- Switch off lights when you leave a room.
- Turn off appliances like TVs, computers, games consoles and DVD machines at the mains; don't leave on 'stand-by'. We, in Britain, waste nearly £1 billion worth of fuel every year by leaving the red lights on.

Kitchen

- Use your washing machine at 30 or 40°C instead of 60°C and only when you have a full load, or select a half-load economy setting.
- Don't use the tumble dryer; hang washing outdoors or on airers in the bathroom.
- Don't leave the fridge or freezer door open longer than necessary and never put warm foods in either.
- Don't over-fill your fridge or freezer; it will have to work harder to maintain the right temperature.
- Defrost your fridge and freezer regularly. A thick build-up of ice will stop it working efficiently.
- Boil only as much water as you need in the kettle.
- Put lids on pans when boiling water – it will heat quicker.
- Never put just one item in the oven – fill it up. For example, if you are cooking a casserole, put some potatoes and a pudding in the oven at the same time. You can even cook root vegetables in the oven in a covered dish with a little water too. If using canned vegetables, take off the paper, open the tin and stand it on the shelf in the oven for the last 10–15 minutes to heat through. Also, when your oven is on to cook a meal, that's the time to use up leftover bread to make melba toast or bruschetta (see page 92).
- If using a pan to boil, say, potatoes, put a steamer or metal colander over the top to steam another vegetable or cook several vegetables together or in separators in a large pan.
- Use a slow cooker, microwave oven, electric grill (broiler), pressure cooker or steamer rather than a conventional oven, when suitable, as they use far less fuel.

10

Getting around

We are, for the most part, lazy nowadays. We get in our cars even to travel a few hundred metres without once thinking of the cost in fuel, to the environment or to our health.

> **Did you know..?** According to National Statistics, carbon emissions in Britain have fallen overall between 1970 and 2003 – but emissions from transport nearly doubled over the same period.

Next time you grab your car keys, stop and think. Do you really need to get in it? Just walking down the road to get your paper or to take the kids to a local school will make a huge difference to your carbon footprint. If you hate walking, get a bicycle. Not such a daft idea; it tones up your muscles, gets your heart pumping and burns more calories than walking (unless you stride out really briskly).

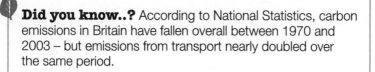

> **Did you know..?** Oil from 3 million cars is wasted every year – that's enough to supply the energy needs for 1.5 million people (Scottish Oil Care Campaign). See page 131 for how to recycle it.

Public transport

I hardly dare mention it but, if public transport is available and reliable, it makes perfect sense to be transporting loads of people using one engine than each of them in separate vehicles. Lucky you if you live in a city with plenty of buses, trams or underground stations nearby – and you should be ashamed of yourself if you use your car all the time on your own. But if you live in the countryside it can be a different matter with little or no public transport provision. This, coupled with train fares rising at an alarming rate, means not using your car for essential journeys is simply unviable for many people until the infrastructure is in place to offer clean, safe, reliable public transport for everyone.

That said, I would still encourage you to use your car only when really necessary, and you should take steps to reduce your carbon emissions from your use of transport and, certainly, use the train instead of a plane whenever you can.

Top tips to lessen the impact of your car

It's madness to expect everyone to rush out and buy a new greener car (though I'll take a look at what's on offer later in the chapter). But, even if you have a gas-guzzler, you can still take steps to ease its impact.

- Drive smoothly (and enjoy the purr of your engine) instead of excessive use of the accelerator and brake.
- Switch to cruise control, if you have it.
- Check your tyre pressures; if they are too soft you'll use more fuel.
- Have your car serviced regularly. In between, check the air filters are clean; if they are dirty they will increase your fuel consumption. They are easy to change following the instructions in your handbook, or pop in to your local garage. It is not an expensive operation.
- Check your mpg readout (if you have one) – you'll soon see at what stages in your driving you use far more fuel than is desirable (obviously, if you're driving up a steep hill, there is nothing you can do but, if it's because of erratic driving, there's really no excuse).
- Switch off air conditioning.

- Come out of gear and put on the handbrake at traffic lights (particularly if you aren't first in the queue).
- Switch off the engine when waiting at level crossings or when waiting to pick up a passenger.
- Travel within the speed limit. Lots of people will tell you that the optimum speed for the most economic use of fuel is 50 mph on a traffic-free road. It isn't as simple as that but you will get lower consumption than when travelling at 60, 70 or more.
- Offset your carbon emissions. I've mentioned www.carbonneutral.com, which I use, but you could also go to www.climatecare.org, the other well-known site. Some new car packages are also offering you the chance to offset up to a year's emissions as part of the deal.
- Recycle your old motor oil when you change the oil in your car. Take it to an oil bank. Call freephone 0800 66 33 66 to find your nearest site. Follow the Oil Care Code – go to www.oilbankline.org.uk.
- Share your car. Organise a lift share yourself or become part of a network. Go to www.liftshare.org to register and see if you can find a 'budi'.

Car clubs

If you don't need a car every day (and many of us don't), you could join a car club. For an annual or monthly membership, you have the use of a car as and when you need it. You can book days, hours or just minutes in advance. You pick it up and drop it off at a designated spot, unlocking it with your membership smart key. The annual fee is less than the cost of an average tax disc and you just pay as you go for fuel, etc. For more information and to see if there is a club near you go to www.carplus.org.

Greener cars

If you are buying a new or secondhand car, consider what's right for you. Here are some basic suggestions but, for a comprehensive guide, go to www.green-car-guide.com and download its guide for less than £5 (with a money-back guarantee).

- **Engine size:** as a general rule, the higher the cubic capacity of the engine, the more it will cost to run. So think what you really need.

- **Fuel type:** diesel, petrol, electric, hybrid or alternative fuel. Diesel is more economical than petrol, but dearer to buy and has higher emissions. For the others, see the breakdown below.

- **Carbon emissions:** even if you are buying a secondhand car, you can look up its estimated emissions to give you a guide.

- **Tax bracket:** the government has introduced a graduated vehicle excise duty for cars built after March 2001 according to their emissions; so the higher the emissions, the more you pay.

- **Reliability:** it's no good buying a car that is going to cost you a fortune at the garage.

Alternative fuels

There is a range of new fuels that have been and are being developed as the fuels of the future. They are promoted as being cleaner, having significant benefits for the environment, and being cheaper in the long run. However, there are growing concerns, particularly with the biofuels, that, although they emit less carbon, they create a lot in production; also that, in view of the shortage of food worldwide, it may not be as environmentally friendly as we think to make land over for growing fuel crops instead of food.

Some of the new fuels are really only suitable for commercial use, and you can't necessarily just put those compatible with domestic vehicles in your tank instead of your usual petrol – modifications may need to be made. Some new car models are being manufactured that use the new fuels. Check with your car manufacturer or garage before you do anything but, if you want to know if you can even obtain any of the new fuels in your area, go to the Energy Saving Trust website (see page 152).

Biodiesel

This is made from recycled cooking oil and the oils of various plants like rapeseed, sunflowers and soya beans. It is sold here as E590, which is a blend of 5 per cent biodiesel and 95 per cent normal, low-sulphur diesel. Some studies have shown that the lubricant properties of the mixed fuel are better than those of standard diesel. A minus is that smog-making nitrogen oxides are slightly higher in biodiesel than the normal, low-sulphur one. Check with your manufacturer before using it, but I am told that all warranty their engines to use up to 5 per cent biodiesel and some up to 30 per cent. It is becoming increasingly available on garage forecourts. It is recommended that, soon after you switch to E590, you change the fuel filters as the gunk from years of the old fuel will be flushed through and you may need to do it more than once before you have a really cleanly fuelled car. It should reduce your carbon emissions by 3 per cent in a 5 per cent mix. I still stress that you should check with your manufacturer before you switch.

Bioethanol

This is made from plant matter – sugar (beet and/or cane), starch (such as wheat, cassava or corn) and cellulose (trees). It is fermented to produce ethanol alcohol (additives are put in to stop it being consumed as a drink!). A 5 per cent blend, called E228, can be used in all petrol cars (but check with your manufacturer first) and gives a 3.5 per cent carbon emission reduction. It is available at a limited number of outlets but you may need to do some research as it isn't well advertised yet. The higher blend, called E85, is widely used in the USA and is on the increase in the UK, and will give a reduction in emissions of 50 per cent. In Brazil, 45 per cent of cars are fuelled by it.

Cars are being manufactured to run on it and may cost you up to £500 more than a standard model. Running costs will be much the same.

Pure plant oils (PPOs)

These are made from filtered rapeseed, palm or nut oil (or recycled cooking oil). The reduction in carbon emissions depends on the manufacturing process but they should produce fewer emissions than biodiesel. Manufacturers in the UK will not warranty cars to use PPOs because they have to have a modification – a heater has to be applied to the fuel pipe to increase flow. There is a limited supply at this time but it is set to change. The manufacturing costs are low and cars can be converted or built to use it. It is already established in Germany.

Liquified petroleum gas (LPG)

This is suitable for small cars and vans. It can be made from methane or a mixture of butane and propane, produced as a by-product of oil refining. It works exactly like unleaded petrol but will reduce carbon emissions by up to 15 per cent, compared with petrol, and fuel costs by about 30 per cent. Existing cars will need modifying to take it, at an estimated cost of between £1,200 and £2,700 depending on the car. There are two minuses: the fuel tank is bigger, so you lose a bit of boot space; and LPG-fuelled vehicles are not (yet) allowed through the Channel Tunnel, but this is being reviewed. If you use the Tunnel a lot, you'd better wait and check before you take the plunge.

Fuel cell

These electro-chemical devices use oxygen and hydrogen to make electricity. They can be 'pure' or 'hybrid'. The hybrid, like other electric cars, includes a battery to enable regenerative braking (it reserves energy in this battery when stopping, to use when it re-starts), which can reduce fuel costs by up to 40 per cent. They are not commercially available yet, but I believe manufacturers such as Ford, GM, Honda, Toyota and Mercedes-Benz already have prototypes.

Other non-domestic fuels

Natural gas, biogas and hydrogen are all being developed for use in commercial transportation.

Electric and hybrid cars

I mentioned fuel cells above, but electric and hybrid cars are already in production. They produce no carbon emissions.

Electric vehicles (EVs) simply have a large rechargeable battery which is connected to an electric engine that powers the wheels.

The biggest drawbacks are that most can go only a limited distance (50–100 km/30–60 miles) before recharging, and they are so silent they can be a risk because pedestrians and cyclists don't hear them coming. The battery can be plugged into a normal socket but it takes time to recharge. Some councils are installing recharging sites in their car parks and, in inner London, some on-street plug-in sites are being installed.

The biggest plusses are that they do not incur vehicle excise duty; they cost only about 1p per mile to run; they are exempt from the London Congestion Charge; they are eligible for discounted central London parking; and there are tax benefits.

The big (or little) five are the Reva G-Wiz, the Sakura Maranello 4, the Nice Mega City, the Micro-Vett Ydea, and the Elettrica.

Hybrid electric vehicles (HEVs) have an electric and petrol or diesel engine. When they travel at low speed, they can use just the electric power but, when you accelerate, they provide the boost of the petrol or diesel. This means they use less conventional fuel than ordinary cars and so produce fewer carbon emissions. They usually have regenerative braking (see Fuel Cell, page 134), which saves a lot of fuel too. The engine also cuts out when idling at lights or level crossings, thus saving more energy. They cost considerably more than their conventional cousins but have huge fuel benefits – they average about 55 mpg (5.1 litres per 100 km) and will save about a third on fuel. They recharge as you drive, so you just top up with petrol or diesel as normal (but not so often!). Maintenance is similar to an ordinary car but you have to take it to a garage that has the special diagnostic equipment to check the motor and battery.

The main additional plusses are reduced vehicle excise duty, exemption from the London Congestion Charge, and tax benefits.

The main contenders for hybrid models are the Honda Civic, the Toyoto Prius and the Lexus GS 450h.

11

Conservation, leisure and money

This is a bit of an odds and ends chapter. I wanted to look a little bit at what's happening to our wildlife; at the countryside and how we can all help to protect it; at holidays and leisure activities as families, thinking about where we go and what we do; and, lastly, if you are investing all this care in the future, if any money you are also investing can do some good in the world as well as increase your own wealth.

Wildlife in your own back garden

I am not going to talk about every endangered wild species in Britain but will instead stick to what you might find at home.

 Did you know..? The RSPB says putting out food in winter saves the lives of probably about a million garden birds each year. Ideally, put it out early in the morning and late in the evening when they need it most. Don't put out big bits in spring because it could choke chicks. Clean the site or feeder (just with boiled water) or salmonella can develop.

Birds

To encourage a wide range of birds to come to your garden, balcony or window sill, put out a variety of food. This can be put on a bird table, in a feeder or directly on a window sill or balcony. It can include:

- Raw peanuts (from a reputable source to ensure they don't contain aflatoxins). Put out whole in a feeder or crushed on a bird table or tray.
- Sunflower seeds (preferably without husks so they don't create a mess for you).
- Seed mixes.
- Millet and other cereal grains.
- Fresh coconut (split a whole nut in half, drill a hole in it and hang it from a tree or the balcony). Don't use desiccated (shredded) as it would swell up in the birds' stomachs.
- Fat: when it's cold in winter and early spring, birds need plenty of protein and fat. Smear fat straight on your balcony rail with some seeds, or melt hard fat and dip bread in it, leave it to harden, then put out (or dip the bread in leftover oil). Chopped bacon rind, grated hard cheese, a chunk of hard dripping or animal fat, hung from a branch, can also be given to them.
- Food scraps: bread, soaked in water first (so it doesn't swell up in their stomachs), cooked rice and potatoes. Don't put out mouldy bread or cakes, salty foods or alcoholic ones.
- Dried fruit.
- Pieces of apple.

Always put out water too, preferably in a bird bath or some similar shallow container, so they can drink and bathe.

Make a bird cake

Melt half a block of lard or some dripping in a pan. Leave to cool but not set. Add any of the foods suggested opposite, such as cooked rice, chopped raw peanuts, seeds, some grated cheese and dried fruit. Pour the mixture into a small basin and, when cold, put in the fridge to set hard. Turn out on to a bird table or balcony or wedge in a tree branch. Make sure you position it well away from where cats might lurk.

Note: If small children are making this, don't melt the fat but let it soften at room temperature and get them to squash everything together with their hands. Put a hole in the base of a plastic pot, push the string through and tie a knot on the inside to stop it coming out. Pack the mixture into the pot and hang the whole thing up. Small birds will peck at it from underneath.

For more information about birds go to the Royal Society for the Protection of Birds website (see page 154).

Hedgehogs

Hedgehogs are in decline for several reasons, including the increased use of pesticides in farms and gardens; the loss of their natural habitat in country hedgerows and rough grass at the sides of fields; and more impenetrable gardens (we use more solid fences and walls instead of hedges between properties).

Hedgehogs are a gardener's friend. Although they eat beneficial earthworms, their main diet is beetles and caterpillars. They appreciate a saucer of meaty cat or dog food (not in gravy), cooked minced (ground) chicken (without bones), beef or lamb and always some water – but never put out bread and milk; they can't digest it properly. They also like snacks of unsweetened muesli, banana, raisins, crushed digestive biscuits (graham crackers), bran or crushed crunchy cat or dog biscuits.

They are inquisitive creatures and, if they smell food, will go after it, so don't leave open cans or yoghurt pots lying around the garden – a hedgehog could get its snout stuck in one very easily.

Make sure they can't fall into ponds or swimming pools and check there is somewhere in your garden for them to nest, such as a pile of leaves, logs, straw or brushwood. You can also build a more permanent hedgehog home. For this and more hedgehog

information, contact the British Hedgehog Preservation Society
(see page 151).

Foxes, bats and squirrels

Some people call them vermin: others, like me, love them. That
doesn't mean I like foxes rummaging in my dustbin, squirrels
digging up my bulbs or bats coming into my house by mistake
and freaking me out by flying into the table lamps! But they are
all amazing creatures and there are ways of living side by side
with them.

Foxes

Obviously, if you keep chickens, other birds or small pets outside,
you must keep them shut up at night or the nocturnal fox will get
them. There is no evidence that they attack cats, but rabbits are
another matter. And, though I am not going to debate the fox
hunting issue in the countryside, it is true that there are now many
more foxes killing many more chickens.

But, for the purposes of this book, I am concentrating on urban
foxes. The red fox has adapted incredibly well to its new
surroundings. It eats small mammals, birds, fruit and carrion
(dead meat to you and me). If you choose to encourage them in
your garden, then pet food or fruit would be their choices.
However, I advise you to keep your dustbins closed and don't
leave black plastic sacks of any waste containing food on the
ground or unprotected.

If you want to deter them from your garden, I am reliably
informed that if you get someone (preferably a man) to wee
around the perimeter of the garden, that scent stakes his claim to
the territory and the fox will remain outside it. (If that is just too
embarrassing or otherwise not possible, you could pee into a
container and then pour it around outside!)

Create a wildlife haven in your garden

I'm not going to go into great detail but just consider the sort of environment you could create.

- Plant shrubs and flowers that attract insects, such as butterflies, hoverflies and bees for their nectar. Some of the best garden plants are buddleia (butterflies love it), cotoneasters, hostas, irises, marigolds, michaelmas daisies, ornamental grasses, phlox, pyracanthas, sunflowers and sweet williams.
- Have a wild corner and sow mixed wild flowers from seeds (if you keep them in a specific area, you won't pull them up by mistake when weeding), but also let some nettles grow (in a controlled fashion) and any flowering weeds that come up can stay with the wild flowers.
- Where possible, have flowering hedges instead of having fences or walls. They encourage nesting birds, hedgehogs, voles and shrews.
- Build a rockery. Female frogs, toads and newts will love it in winter. If you can build it round a small ornamental pond, then so much the better. Have a gradual slope made of stones or concrete (not plastic) along one side so wildlife can come to drink without falling in and make sure it's not under a tree that will shed its leaves, pine cones or seeds in autumn.
- Make bird or hedgehog homes (see page 139 for details of the sort of habitat they like and also the relevant organisations for information about permanent homes).
- Don't use chemical slug pellets or fertilisers; there are plenty of organic compounds available. The old-fashioned idea of putting cups of beer down to kill slugs does work – but might also harm your hedgehogs! Putting scooped-out orange or grapefruit shells or just the peel between the plants seems to stop a lot of slugs. Spraying with eco-friendly washing-up liquid and water also stops aphids.
- As said in the water chapter, don't use sprinklers or a hosepipe – they waste huge amounts of water. Collect water in your water butt and use to water the plants. Don't water the grass even when it goes brown in the summer; it will recover perfectly well when it rains again.

Bats

Bats are a protected species and it is illegal to harm them in any way, and you shouldn't disturb them either. They cause no harm. They don't even build nests; they creep into dark corners and crevices. You'll mostly see them between May and September when the mothers will be rearing their babies. Bat poo, by the way, makes a very good fertiliser! Be careful about putting down poison for wasps, rats, mice or flies if you know bats are in the vicinity. For more information about these fascinating creatures, contact the Bat Conservation Trust (see page 151). If you need help with one or more specific bats, call its helpline on 0845 1300 228.

Squirrels

The red squirrel is an endangered species but the grey squirrel is thriving! Although it is delightful to watch them jumping through the woods at a distance, they are a pest in woodlands and are becoming so in some homes. It is important to make sure they can't get into your loft as they can chew cables, eat insulation material and generally create mayhem! Block up any holes and quickly replace slipped tiles on the roof (particularly if it isn't lined – though it should be for insulation purposes). If they are becoming a nuisance, you'll have to stop putting out food for the birds as it will attract squirrels too.

Eco-friendly garden furniture

This is just a postscript really, but I felt it had to be said. When choosing garden furniture, consider what it's made of. You could go for lovely wooden tables and chairs, made from reclaimed teak (www.arborvetum.co.uk) or check out B&Q, Wyevale, Tesco, Asda and M&S – the top five according to Greenpeace's garden furniture league table for 2006 for stocking only wooden furniture that's FSC approved (see page 75 for the logo). Alternatively, go for recycled plastic; (www.marmaxproducts.co.uk or www.playquest. co.uk are two mail-order websites).

Patio heaters

These outdoor metal monstrosities burn enough fuel to make 400 cups of tea in an hour and waste energy as the majority of the heat goes straight up into the sky. It is estimated that they create

140,000 tonnes of carbon emissions per year. The EU is looking at efficiency standards that will be applied to them. It won't ban them but the standards are likely to be so stringent that none will meet them. So, hopefully, they will soon become a thing of the past. Curry's has already stopped selling them, and B&Q has said it will stop selling them as soon as the present stocks are gone. Others will follow suit. Pub-visiting smokers are up in arms because these heaters keep them warm while they are puffing outside the pub in the wind and rain. Sorry, but I don't really have any sympathy; they'll just have to put on recycled plastic fleeces instead!

Respect the countryside

As an environmentally conscious person, you'll be well aware that there is a Countryside Code to follow. I'm just going to recap here, no more.

Five steps to the Countryside Code

1. **Be safe, plan ahead and follow any signs.**
   - Be aware that some areas of open land may be restricted while safety works are carried out or because it is the breeding season for a specific species or farm animals.
   - Always read and follow signs that have been put up to inform you of diversions or about how to behave. Learn the signs and symbols used in the countryside so you can act accordingly.
   - Use an up-to-date map or guide book.
   - Check weather conditions before you set out and choose your clothing and footwear accordingly.
   - Make sure someone knows where you are going and how long you plan to be. Even if you carry a mobile phone, you may be in an area with no signal!
2. **Leave gates and property as you find them.**
   - Farmers allow you to cross their land but you have to respect that their livestock needs protecting. If you leave gates open that should be shut, they can stray: if you shut them when they were open, you could prevent the animals reaching food or water. Make sure the last person through a gate knows how to leave it.
   - Follow the public footpath; don't stray on to private land.

- In fields of crops, stick to the edge unless a sign tells you to do otherwise.
- If you see a makeshift sign that says, for instance 'Private, no entry' and it is clearly on a public footpath, report it. The respect works both ways!
- Use gates or stiles; don't push through hedges or bend wire fences.
- Don't disturb heritage sites or ruins or take part of them as souvenirs.
- Leave farm machinery and livestock alone. If you see an animal in distress, try to find the farmer.

3. **Protect plants and animals and take your litter home.**
   - Don't damage or remove plants, rocks or trees. They not only provide enjoyment for us, they are also the natural habitat and food for many creatures great and small.
   - Give wild animals and farm livestock plenty of space. They can be unpredictable. Never run or shout near them. Walk quietly and calmly.
   - Don't drop litter. Not only is it unsightly, it can be dangerous to livestock and the environment. It is a criminal offence to dump any rubbish in a public place.
   - Fires can be devastating. Never drop cigarette or cigar ends. Even if you think you've put it out, it could still be smouldering and potentially start a fire. If you see a fire, check, first, if it is a controlled one (particularly on heath and moor land) as between October and April they are used as a way to manage vegetation and rejuvenate the soil. If you think it is an unscheduled fire, call 999.

4. **Keep dogs under control.**
   - It is illegal to let your dog run free near farm animals all year round and on common and open land between 1 March and 30 September.
   - You don't have to keep your dog on the lead on public paths as long as it is under control. If you know your dog is not obedient, keep it on a lead. If your dog worries farm animals such as sheep, the farmer is entitled to shoot it.
   - Be aware in the lambing season that your dog must be kept well under control and also if you know birds nest in the area or other animals are breeding. A dog can easily frighten off the parents and the offspring can die if unprotected.

- Always take a pooper scooper and a bag – NEVER leave dog mess. Also make sure your dog is regularly wormed. This is an extra precaution in case it runs off and poos in the undergrowth where you are unaware of it.
- If you see signs asking you to keep your dog on a lead, obey them unquestioningly. They will be there for very good reason, most probably because of breeding animals or new plant growth.

5. **Consider other people.**
   - If you are driving in the countryside, don't speed, rev your engine or brake suddenly. Where possible, leave your car at home, take a train or bus or ride a bike. If you do take your car, park it sensibly, not blocking gateways or driveways or in private fields.
   - When driving a car or riding a bike, slow down for horses, walkers and livestock and give them a wide berth. By law, cyclists must give way to horseriders and walkers on a bridlepath.
   - Don't play loud music in your car or when having a picnic.
   - Support local farmers and buy their produce.

Holidays and leisure

Making that trip

We've already discussed transport but, if you are considering taking a plane rather than a train or coach (much more eco-friendly options), at least think about offsetting your part of the carbon emissions for the journey (see pages 20–21).

I love travelling and don't think I shall stop going abroad. There is so much to see and learn. However, when you are planning a holiday, think about the environment you are going to. Has the area been destroyed and the locals uprooted just to build concrete jungles for tourism? Or has it been done tastefully and in an environmentally conscious way? There are eco-friendly resorts springing up all over the world. I visited one in Mexico and it was wonderful. There were salt water, solar-heated showers; water-powered electricity; local produce to eat; and it was situated right on the beach in very comfortable thatched huts.

Some people argue that these so-called eco-friendly resorts are just jumping on a trendy bandwagon. Well, that's for you to decide. If you key 'eco-friendly resort' into your search engine, you will see the whole range that is available. Alternatively, talk to your travel agent.

In the UK you'll find many resorts and hotels that offer eco-friendly facilities. One thing I implore you, go to places where good local produce is offered and, if given the chance to be eco-friendly (such as keeping your towels for a few nights rather than being given new ones every day), go with it. Forget the idea that as you are paying for this service you are entitled to it – hotel laundries are hugely environmentally unfriendly. I suspect those who insist on these unnecessary luxuries are the same people that pinch all the toiletries, writing paper and even the bath robes!

Leisure activities

If your kids' idea of entertainment is playing computer games all day or being given the money to go to the cinema or to a chain pizza restaurant, why not try to get them to think differently? For better alternatives for their health and your pocket, why not try some of the following?

- Take them to the local park with some friends and play five-a-side football, frisbee, catch, short tennis or cricket.

- Set up an assault course in the garden and time them to see who can get round the quickest. You can have different 'stations' with an activity at each. Perhaps they have to run along a ladder laid on the ground, then pick up a ball (or several) to throw into a bucket, then balance on a set of stepping stones (you can use bricks, stones or even books on a dry day), walk along a piece of string or tape on the ground, do a somersault over a large cushion, stack up a pile of small plant pots, run up a plank balancing on a low log, so it see-saws and they run down the other side. The options depend on what you have to hand but there will always be something you can use.

- Teach them to play Kick the Can. All but one goes and hides, having decided where 'home' is. As the person who is 'it' seeks them out, they try to race past them and reach home without being caught.

- Take them to a pick-your-own farm. You'll find they really enjoy picking (and eating!) the fruit and, if you pick vegetables like peas, there's more fun to be had with the shelling afterwards. Get them to help with the produce later, either preparing it for the freezer, making jam or whatever else you like to do (see Preserving on pages 103–109).

- Play Sardines in the house. One person goes and hides in a place where others can squeeze in. The others search and, as they find the person, they squeeze in too until only one person is left.

- Go on a family jog. No one is allowed to walk, even if the pace is still quite slow.

- Go on a nature ramble. You each have a list of natural things to search for and as you walk through the countryside or your local park and find them you tick them off the list. You don't have to do it as an individual activity; everyone should call out when they find something so everyone can admire it (make sure you don't frighten wildlife or pick flowers, etc. though).

- An environmentally friendly pastime is a litter pick. Give them gloves to wear and strict instructions not to pick up any glass, needles or other potentially dangerous litter (each child should be supervised anyway). They could look for something beginning with each letter of the alphabet or just take bags and see who can pick up the most in a set time. Then sort it and dispose of it either in your recycling bins or in the dustbin, as appropriate.

- Have a Hunt My Trail. One person sets off and leaves a trail with arrows or other signs made of twigs, stones, etc. After an agreed time, the others follow the trail and try to find the person hiding at the end. Make sure small children are supervised and that everyone knows the agreed place to meet again if they don't find the person.

- Go rockpooling/fishing/shrimping on a suitable beach or search for fossils and shells. If you find shells, take them home and make a shell picture. Only collect fossils from public beaches. Don't go near cliff faces or rock falls – for safety reasons and also because you would need to have permission from the cliff owner to take away any fossils you found there. The best time to search is when the tide is on its way out.

- Take the family on a cycle ride. Pack drinks and snacks or even a picnic and set off. Even city-dwellers can cycle to a park.

- Teach your kids to cook. Making biscuits (cookies), little pastry (paste) tarts or fairy cakes are great fun to start with. Fairy cakes cooked in the microwave are the best as they can be watched magically rising before your very eyes. Make a normal quick sponge mixture with 50 g/2 oz each of soft butter, light brown sugar and self-raising flour. Add ½ a teaspoonful of baking powder and 1 large egg and beat well with a wooden spoon until light and fluffy. Put 6 or 7 double-thickness paper cake cases (cupcake papers) in a circle on the microwave turntable and half-fill with the mixture. Microwave on High for 1½–3 minutes (depending on the output of your microwave) until risen and shrinking away from the sides slightly but still very slightly wet on top. Remove and leave to cool, then ice or decorate as required. For chocolate ones, replace a heaped tablespoonful of the flour with a heaped tablespoonful of cocoa (unsweetened chocolate) powder.

Caring about your money

If you are investing money instead of putting it under your mattress, you must want it to make a profit. But do you care where that profit comes from? Our increasing awareness of our responsibilities to other countries and people as well as our planet is making a difference to the way we invest. You can now buy mortgages and pensions and take out bank accounts and investments that all have ethical principles.

In a 3-month period in spring/summer 2007, we in the UK invested nearly £140 million in ethical funds – that was up by about 80 per cent on the same period the previous year and it has been rapidly increasing each quarter since, according to the Investment Management Association.

Although I am no investment broker, this should just give you a little food for thought.

What are ethical companies?

These are, in theory, those that are environmentally aware – and are seen to be. For instance: cosmetic companies that don't test their products on animals; wood suppliers that plant more trees than they chop down; or those with a well-publicised human rights ethic. One noted advantage often quoted is that they may be less likely to be affected by boycotts, strikes and financially embarrassing court cases, all of which can have a bad effect on their share price. Some people also feel that their focus on sustainability should give them better long-term prospects. For example, that same wood supplier will have an endless supply of trees but a less ethical one that cuts down more than it grows, will run out!

Other prospects might be alternative power suppliers, like wind turbine companies (it's never going to stop being windy!) or, perhaps, large recycling consortiums. As with any financial decision, you should weigh up all the evidence and take appropriate advice.

How to make ethical investments

Friends Provident pioneered ethical investing back in 1984 and is one of the leaders today for investment funds and pensions. It is difficult to judge which companies are ethically sound without the necessary experience to plough through all the jargon so, for most of us, it's advisable to invest in them through Open Ended Investment Companies (OEICs) and Unit Trusts, through a managed fund. These are much the same things really, but OEICs have many sub-funds under one umbrella, from which you can swap to and fro as circumstances change without incurring a charge. You buy a portfolio of shares but, before you decide, the ethical fund manager will check out the companies to see if they meet a number of acceptable or unacceptable criteria. It isn't always that cut and dried, though. For instance, you may feel strongly about the work of a pharmaceutical company finding a cure for cancer and want to invest in it – but discover that it also tests its drugs on animals. So it might all depend on your stand on vivisection.

Acceptable criteria:

- High involvement in recycling and conservation.
- Serious commitment to reducing their carbon footprint.
- Pollution reduction and control.
- Specific environmental protection policies.
- Best human rights practices re. employment, trade unions and treatment of workers, both in their own workforce and with whom they trade.

Unacceptable criteria:

- Environmentally damaging products.
- Arms or nuclear weapon manufacture.
- Human or animal exploitation.
- Support of oppressive regimes.
- Gambling or pornography.
- Promotion of alcohol or tobacco.

For more information on ethical investing and other money matters, go to www.thisismoney.co.uk or ask your own financial adviser. For one in your area specialising in ethical investments, go to www.unbiased.co.uk. Another good source of much more detailed information than I have given here is the Ethical Investment Research Service (EIRIS, see page 152).

Other money matters

It is possible to become as green as your bank notes and find an ethical bank, building society, mortgage supplier and pension plan. You can even move your insurances to more ethically friendly companies. The EIRIS publishes a list of ethical financial advisers, and leaflets on a range of ethical financial matters. The Co-operative Bank is a good place to start or you could check out Marks & Spencer Financial Services.

Useful addresses

Action Network
www.bbc.co.uk/dna/actionnetwork

Association of Children's Hospices
First Floor, Canningford House,
38 Victoria Street, Bristol, BS1 6BY
0117 989 7820
info@childhospice.org.uk
www.childhospice.org.uk

Barnardo's
Tanners Lane, Barkingside, Ilford,
Essex, IG6 1QG
020 8550 8822
dorothy.howes@barnardos.org.uk
www.barnados.org.uk

Bat Conservation Trust
Unit 2, 15 Cloisters House, 8 Battersea
Park Road, London, SW8 4BG
0845 1300 288
www.bats.org.uk

BigBarn
www.bigbarn.co.uk

Brita Recycling
FREEPOST, NAT17876, Bicester,
OX26 4BR

British Gas
0845 675 0604
www.britishgas.co.uk

British Hedgehog Preservation Society
Hedgehog House, Dhustone, Ludlow,
Shropshire SY8 3PL
01584 890801
www.britishhedgehogs.org.uk

Carbon Footprint
www.carbonfootprint.com

CarbonNeutral Company
www.carbonneutral.com

Community Recycling Network UK
57 Prince Street, Bristol. BS1 4QH
0117 942 0142
info@crn.org.uk
www.crn.org.uk

Coopers of Stortford
01279 656 551
www.coopersofstortford.co.uk

Curtain Exchange
www.thecurtainexchange.net

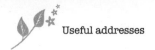

DefraUK
08459 33 55 77
helpline@defra.gsi.gov.uk
www.defra.gsi.gov.uk

**Department of the Environment's
Tidy Northern Ireland Campaign**
To report fly-tipping in Northern
Ireland.
0845 3000 630

Don'tDumpThat
www.dontdumpthat.com

**Draught Proofing Advisory
Association**
PO Box 12, Haslemere, Surrey,
GU27 3AH
01428 654011

Eaga Partnership
The Warm Front Scheme Manager
Freephone: 0800 316 6011

eBay
www.ebay.co.uk

Eco Balls
c/o Fraser Simpson Associates Limited
Unit 4 Stonestile Business Park
Stonestile Road, Headcorn, Kent,
TN27 9PG
0800 107 7213
www.ecoballsdirect.co.uk

Ecover
www.ecover.com

Energy Efficiency Advice Centre
0800 512 012

Energy Saving Advice Centre
0800 512 012

Energy Saving Trust
0800 512 012
www.energysavingtrust.org.uk

Environment Agency
0800 807060 (to report fly-tipping in
England and Wales)
www.environment-agency.gov.uk

**Environmental Campaigns
(ENCAMS)**
www.encams.org

Ethical Consumer **magazine**
www.ethicalconsumer.org

Ethical Investment Research Service
80–84 Bondway, London, SW8 1SF
020 7840 5700
www.eiris.org

Ethical Superstore
www.ethicalsuperstore.com

The Fairtrade Foundation
Room 204, 16 Baldwin's Gardens,
London, EC1N 7RJ
020 7405 5942
mail@fairtrade.org.uk
www.fairtrade.org.uk

Food from Britain
www.foodfrombritain.co.uk

The Foody
www.thefoody.com

Friends of the Earth
26–28 Underwood Street,
London, N1 7JQ
020 7490 1555
www.foe.co.uk

Furniture Re-use Network
0117 954 3571
www.frn.org.uk

GHS Recycling Ltd
(Linda Renwick)
32 Ackworth Road, Shawcross
Industrial Park, Hilsea, Portsmouth,
Hants, PO3 5JP
02392 670399
linda@ghsrecyclingltd.co.uk

Green Providers Directory
www.search-for-me.co.uk
This directory lists a range of eco-
friendly charities and organisations
dedicated to protecting wildlife and
habitats, helping endangered species,
saving rainforests and alleviating
poverty in third world countries. For a
small donation you can make a real
difference. You can even buy a piece of
rainforest and protect it for life.

GreenChoices
www.greenchoices.org

Green Stationery Company
www.greenstat.co.uk

Greenpeace
Canonbury Villas, London, N1 2PN
020 7865 8100
www.greenpeace.org.uk
Greenpeace supporters are a powerful
voice, finding environmentally
responsible solutions to climate
change, protecting the planet and
exposing environmental abuse.

The Guardian
For news and information on the
environment go to
www.guardianunlimited.co.uk/
environment

Heat Pump Association
www.heatpumps.org.uk

Help the Aged Stamp Appeal
36A Bunkers Hill, Romiley, Stockport
SK6 3DS

The Laundry CD Recycling
London Recycling, 4d North Crescent,
Cody Road, London, E16 4TG

Mailing Preference Service (MPS)
DMA House, 70 Margaret Street,
London W1W 8SS
0845 703 4599
www.mpsonline.org.uk

**National Association of Nappy
Services**
0121 693 4949
www.changeanappy.co.uk

**National Association of Toy &
Leisure Libraries**
020 7255 4640
www.natll.org.uk

National Customer Contact Centre
PO Box 544, Rotherham, S60 1BY
General enquiries: 08708 506 506
(Mon–Fri 8–6)
Incident hotline: 0800 807060
(24 hours)
enquiries@environment-agency.org.uk

**National Farmers' Retail & Markets
Association**
PO Box 575, Southampton,
SO15 7BZ
0845 45 88 420
www.farmersmarkets.net

Natural Collection
www.naturalcollection.com

OFWAT
www.ofwat.gov.uk

Oxfam
0845 3000 311
support@oxfam.org.uk

Oxfam Bring Bring Scheme
Freepost LON16281,
London, WC1N 3BR
0870 752 0999

Rag-and-Bone
www.rag-and-bone.co.uk

Re-cycle
Unit A, Global Park, Moorside,
Colchester, Essex CO1 2TW
0845 458 0852/01206 863111
www.re-cycle.org

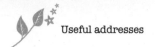

Recycled Paper Supplies
www.rps.gn.apc.org

RNIB Stamp Recycling
PO Box 185, Benfleet, Essex, SS7 9BH

Royal Mail Door to Door Opt Outs
Kingsmead House, Oxpens Road,
Oxford, OX1 1RX
optout@royalmail.com

**Royal Society for the Protection
of Birds**
www.rspb.org.uk

Salvation Army
www.salvationarmy.org.uk
www.satradingco.org

**Scottish Environment Protection
Agency**
To report fly-tipping in Scotland.
0845 30 40 90
www.dumbdumpers.org

Shelter
0845 458 4590
www.england.shelter.org.uk

Soil Association
South Plaza, Marlborough Street,
Bristol, BS1 3NX
0117 314 5000
www.soilassociation.org
www.soilassociationscotland.org
The leading UK promoter of
sustainable organic farming.

Stop Junk Mail Campaign
2 Mill Hill Road, Norwich,
Norfolk, NR2 3DP
01623 618185
www.stopjunkmail.org.uk

Tetra Pak Recycling
c/o Perrys Recycling, Showground
Road, Bridgewater, Somerset
TA6 6AJ
www.tetrapakrecycling.co.uk

Trees for Life
www.treesforlife.org.uk

Woodland Trust
www.woodland-trust.org.uk
www.wt-store.com

Other websites

www.alotoforganics.co.uk – organic vegetable boxes, re-usable nappies
www.arborvetum.co.uk – reclaimed teak garden furniture
www.ashcan.co.uk – portable/disposable ashtrays
www.bikerecycling.org.uk – for bike recycling projects
www.buttless.co.uk – portable/disposable ashtrays
www.buttsandgum.com – portable/disposable ashtrays
www.buttsout.co.uk – portable/disposable ashtrays
www.carplus.org – to locate a car club near you
www.cartridges4causes.co.uk – ink/toner cartridge recycling
www.cleanercitites.co.uk – portable/disposable ashtrays
www.climatecare.org – to offset your carbon emissions
www.co2balance.com – to offset your carbon emissions
www.direct.gov.uk – eligibility for a government home insulation grant
www.direct/gov.uk/actonco2 - the UK government's carbon footprint calculator
www.dirtypig.org – action against littering
www.eattheseasons.co.uk – information on seasonal foods
www.ecotopia.co.uk – eco-friendly household products
www.green-car-guide.com – downloadable guide to greener new and secondhand cars
www.greenerstyle.co.uk – recycled products
www.greenpeople.co.uk – organic skin and hair care
www.greenshop.co.uk – newspaper (and other materials) log makers
www.keeper-com – environmentally friendly feminine hygiene
www.liftshare.org – register of car lift-sharing schemes
www.marmaxroducts.co.uk – recycled plastic garden furniture
www.mooncup.co.uk – environmentally friendly feminine hygiene
www.naturebotts.co.uk – biodegradable nappies
www.oilbankline.org.uk – for the Oil Care Code for disposal of motor oil
www.pchardware.co.uk – information to help you update your computer
www.planettrash.co.uk – recycled products
www.playquest – recycled plastic garden furniture
www.recycledprproducts.org.uk – a guide to products made from recycled materials
www.recycle-more.co.uk – recycling bank locator
www.recyclenow.com – special offers on composting bins
www.recyclingappeal.com/scope – ink/toner cartridge recycling
www.recycling-guide.org.uk – recycling bank locator
www.recycling.tiscali.co.uk – mobile phone recycling
www.restorationservices.co.uk – repairs to dolls, rocking horses and wooden and soft toys
www.reuze.co.uk – the how, what and where of recycling in the UK
www.simplyfair.co.uk – recycled products
www.soorganic.com – eco-friendly household products
www.spiritofnature.co.uk – eco-friendly household products, biodegradable nappies
www.stubbi.net – portable/disposable ashtrays
www.thegreenstoreonline.co.uk – a wide range of environmentally friendly products
www.thelightbulb.co.uk – suppliers of a range of low-energy light bulbs.
www.thisismoney.co.uk – advice on ethical investment
www.toyrepairs.co.uk – repairs to toy bears and dolls
www.toys-to-you.co.uk – ethical kids' playthings
www.ukfoodonline.co.uk – organic vegetable boxes
www.unbiased.co.uk – advice on ethical investment
www.uswitch.com – a site that compares utilities suppliers; it can also assess the
    economics of a water meter in your household
www.wasteonline.org.uk – information and incredible facts about rubbish
www.wellfieldbears.co.uk – repairs to toy bears and dolls
www.wigglywrigglers.co.uk – worms for composting
www.wormsdirect.co.uk – worms for composting

Index